# PLAN
# YOUR WEBSITE

First Published in Great Britain 2015 by
Online Mastery Limited

I dedicate this book to my two girls, Jaime and Lilly. Without them, I simply wouldn't be here today.

# What People Are Saying

Steve is one of the world's leading experts in his field. We run a multi million-dollar company and Steve has personally had a profound impact on the success of our launches. It is rare that you work with someone that provides measurable 1000's of percent return on investment, but Steve truly has for us on many occasions.

*Ben Croft, CEO - WBECS*

This book contains sound marketing ideas for a digital world. It is written for people who are setting up a new business or want to have a better presence online. Even more powerful is the author's story behind the book.

*Daniel Priestley, Entrepreneur and Best-Selling Author*

If you can't get results using this comprehensive guide, you should probably get a job and leave entrepreneurship for others.

*Michael Serwa, High-end Life Coach, Speaker & Author*

I had a website but it wasn't performing. I created a strategy with Steve's help to make my website and online communication more effective. This allowed me to simplify the user experience and double the prices of my digital programs (and sell more)! People's response to my new site has been amazing.

*Jaime Miller, ESL / ELT Teacher Trainer*

I can't tell you the number of clients I've helped since 1995, building websites. It's thousands. If I could do it all again, I would write a book that covered everything they needed to know about building their website. Thankfully, going forward, I just need to point to Steve's incredible book. He's already done all the hard work. The best part is that when I point to it, my clients thank me. Me! Simply for pointing the way to an amazing resource. You should try it.

*Chris Lema, CTO - Crowd Favorite*

Whether creating your own website or getting someone to do it for you, this book is the perfect starting point. Steve shows you how to make your website work for you once it's launched, not just plan it. He explains what you need to know from the techie side, very simply, especially if you are commissioning it, so you know what questions to ask. Great book for entrepreneurs, start-ups and established business owners.

*Baiju Solanki, Founder - Be Entrepreneur Co.*

Plan Your Website is the key to unlocking the unlimited potential of your website. When you know why you're planning and what you need to think about, you have the motivation and the means to make your site work for you 24/7/365 - and that's exactly what Steve Woody delivers in this groundbreaking book.

*Allison Rapp, Business Coach for Hands-On Practitioners*

As a professional online entrepreneur, I have picked up numerous tips in Plan Your Website that I wish I knew when I was starting out. Steve Woody has put together an easy-to-follow plan so any beginner can avoid mistakes and confidently manage developers to ensure their website project comes in on-time and on-budget.

*Sherrie Rose, Founder - The Webinar Way*

I never expected a book about website building to be this fascinating. I have no technical background whatsoever on this and there wasn't a single word or concept I didn't understand. Can't wait to read more! Steve really managed to get me excited about building a website! Unbelievable!

*Nina-Maria Gorgens, Holistic Health Consultant*

This book should be required reading for anyone even contemplating building a website. Whether you're doing it yourself or paying to have it done for you, the results you get will be directly related to how well you follow Steve's PLAN.

*Joe Gregory, Author - How to Write Your Book Without The Fuss*

# Contents

Is this book for you?                                        1
Workbook Download                                           3
The Importance of Your P.L.A.N.                             4

**CHAPTER 1 — STRATEGY**                                    11
Who are you?                                                14
What is your business?                                      16
Who is your Target Audience?                                19
What is your Exit Strategy?                                 24
What is your Timeframe?                                     27
What is your Budget?                                        31
What is Your Online Identity?                               37

**CHAPTER 2 — THE CUSTOMER JOURNEY**                        47
The Opt In                                                  50
Initial Product Offer                                       56
Core Offer                                                  57
Upsells                                                     59

**CHAPTER 3 — SITEMAPS**                                    61
XML Sitemaps                                                62
HTML Sitemap                                                62
Information Architecture                                    62

**CHAPTER 4 — WIREFRAMES**                                  69
Best Practice                                               71
Responsive Design                                           73

**CHAPTER 5 — CONTENT**                                     79
Content for People                                          81
Content for SEO                                             86
Other Content to Consider                                   88
Conclusion                                                  90

**CHAPTER 6 — DESIGN**                                      91
The Purpose of Design                                       92
Branding                                                    92
Consistency                                                 95

Your Logo                                         95
Website Ready Images                              96
Responsive Design                                 97
Copyright Images                                  98
Budget                                            98
When You Contract a Freelance Designer            99
Conclusion                                       100

**CHAPTER 7 — SYSTEMS**                          101
Content Management Systems (CMS)                 102
Hosting                                          105
Customer Relationship Management (CRM)           108
Email                                            108
Auto — Responders                                109
E — commerce                                     110
Membership                                       112
Support                                          112
Page Builders                                    114
Backing Up Your Website                          114
Contact Forms                                    114
API Access                                       116
Cookies                                          117

**CHAPTER 8 — TESTING**                          119
Test the Customer Journey                        121
Test the Functionality                           122

**CHAPTER 9 — ANALYTICS**                        125
Retargeting                                      126
Conversion Pixels                                127
Tag Management                                   128
Heat Map Tracking                                128
Conclusion                                       129

**CHAPTER 10 — SPLIT TESTING**                   131

**WHAT'S NEXT?**                                 135
Congratulations!                                 135
Workbook Download                                135

# Foreword

Relationships in a maturing digital era continue to fascinate me. Steve and I have never met and yet I feel as though I know him well. We may walk right by each other on the street and yet I consider him a friend. While physical location has separated us, the power of technology has allowed for our worlds to become smaller in a way perhaps many of you have experienced in this internet age.

Almost two years ago, Steve became a customer of ours and I could quickly tell we would become fast friends. With a shared passion for technology and people, Steve exhibited to me a near insatiable appetite for learning. And while learning on its own is a noble pursuit, knowledge without application is only part of the equation. I was always struck by Steve's desire to apply the things he was learning, to test them out, to see the results, and then to go back to the proverbial drawing board and write down what he learned.

This commitment to testing, refining, and retesting is so critical in any business pursuit, and it is the results from those tests that comprise the education of this book. You'll discover that Steve's approach to teaching is as much perspective as it is process, and that if you are willing, he can shorten the gap for you between knowledge and application.

At Themeco, we like to focus on a modified version of the Pareto principle or the 80/20 rule that says 20% of your actions will produce 80% of your results. I see Steve's book as just that kind of resource. The years of trial and error, success and failure, highs and lows are consolidated in an easy to digest and entertaining format that when applied will make a difference in your business whether it be new or established.

**Kyle Wakefield,** *Founder of Themeco*

# Is this book for you?

I imagine you are reading this book because you're thinking about creating a website. It could be that you already have one and it is not giving you the results that you desire. Perhaps you have website shame because it's outdated or was designed poorly. Maybe, as I see so often, you started the process and now feel totally overwhelmed or frustrated.

Whatever your reason for picking up this book, I want to assure you that I respect and acknowledge you for taking the time to read what I have to write.

So what makes me qualified to write this book?

Firstly, this book isn't about me; it's about you. My education and life experiences are only important for the purpose of giving you the assurance that your time spent reading this will not be wasted.

I've made many mistakes that have cost me time, money and friendships and whilst my life is still constantly improving, I have to respect that in the past few years I've transformed myself from homeless and unemployed to become the chairman of a non—profit organisation, published author of a bestselling book and director of a successful limited company.

To be successful is not to avoid failure, but to recognise it and overcome the challenges quickly.

*"I know that I am going to be successful because I am running out of things to do wrong"* ~ *Napoleon Hill*

I have been honoured to be coached by the world's leading peak performance expert Tony Robbins and something he talks about is CANI which stands for constant and never—ending improvement.

The improvement of your online presence is something that you should constantly work towards. It is never finished, and as you learn and grow, so will your business. Technology is constantly changing and you need to ensure that you provide a website and functionality that are current.

This book exists because I was struggling to help all the people who were approaching me. Having only twenty—four hours in a day, I needed to find a way to extend myself and this has become one of my biggest lessons in life. Time is our most valuable commodity and, unlike money, it can't be replaced. You, too, need to start setting yourself up to work on your business, not in it.

I can't stress the following enough:
**If you fail to prepare, then prepare to fail.**

Above everything else, you need to know your outcome, understand what you want, and then create a strategy to get you there. This does not need to be set in stone, but it must have the foundational weight to guide you through moments of despair and discouragement. It must contain enough information to navigate you away from common mistakes and towards a successful online presence. Your business must give you the freedom to enjoy the benefits of life.

The intended outcome of reading this book is that you will gain the knowledge necessary to create a strategy that will act as the foundation for your website. With the information contained within this book, you can speak to designers and developers with a better understanding of your requirements, or teach yourself to build your own website through our Academy of Online Mastery.

# Workbook Download

Please visit

http://PlanYourWebsite.co.uk/workbook

or scan the QR code below
to download your FREE workbook.

Your workbook accompanies this book; it gives you step by
step instructions for creating your website strategy

# The Importance of Your P.L.A.N.

Would you jump from a plane without a parachute for ten million pounds?

Chances are you're thinking, NO! There's no point having all that money if I'm not alive to use it.

What if I tell you that the plane would be on the ground when you jump? Are you thinking differently now?

You must always ensure you gather as many facts as possible before making any important decision.

The PLAN is a starting point, not the answer.

The purpose of this chapter is to identify the problems caused by poor planning, how they can affect you and what you can do to eliminate them. Whilst this chapter will speak about the importance of creating your plan, subsequent chapters will show you, step by step, how to create it ... And yes, P.L.A.N. stands for something. I'll cover that later.

I've seen this too many times. I've done it. Desperate for work, trying to earn some money, I would grasp at any opportunity that was set before me. When I first started this business and someone came to me, in need of a website, the conversation sounded something like this:

**Client:** "I need a professional website. I've been let down by my developer and now I don't have much of a budget."

**Me:** "No worries. Let me see what I can do. What is it that you need?"

**Client:** "Just a few pages, some info about the business, social media and a way to contact me."

**Me:** "Sure. I'll do that."

Although my outcome was to complete the work, I was on a journey that would eventually cause me to lose friendships, question my identity and ultimately suffer a breakdown.

It was during this point in my life that the concept of Online Mastery was born.

At whatever stage you find yourself, this book can assist you. Its purpose is to get you to take a step back and view the bigger picture in order to move forward with clarity, creating a solid foundation that will support your business as you grow. You do not need any special skills; just the ability to follow a system and take action.

Will Smith once told a story about how his father told him and his brother to build a wall 16 feet high and 30 feet long. At first, the task seemed impossible but their father instructed them to add one brick every day on the way home from school. Surely enough, after 18 months, they had completed the wall.

A project can seem daunting when you consider its scale, but with small steps, progress can be achieved.

Your website works on the same principle. By the end of this book, you will have addressed the essentials of each individual section required for your PLAN, put it all together, and formulated the strategy for your online presence.

You may think that you don't need to do this but let me assure you, one of the most common mistakes I see people make is to assume that a website developer covers all aspects of the design and build. The word website is associated with technical matters, so it is often presumed that a website designer will not only know how to code your website, but that he or she can assist if your laptop breaks, that they'll understand the instruction manual for your microwave... or how to ensure you never get spammed. (I'm still searching for that answer.)

Assuming this can be dangerous.

The fact is that most people who work online have one specific skill and a limited selection of understandings. Someone who writes code and is known as a developer is usually analytical and uses the left side of their brain, whereas someone who creates brand identities, logos and artwork is likely more visual and uses the creative right side of their brain.

There used to only be four areas to consider when creating a website. These were planning, design, development and marketing. Necessary skills for each element would vary, and to obtain a high standard throughout, they would often require more than one person.

What was once a requirement is no longer true. With the evolution of technology, it is possible to obtain everything you need with little effort and often without hiring multiple people or an agency to manage the build – as long as you know the right places to look. Before I get into that, I want you to consider the following example of why having a plan for your website is so important.

Imagine you ask me to bake a cake.

Maybe I have baked a few cupcakes before and they turned out okay or you remember the nice cream cakes you once saw me eating. I mean seriously... How hard can it really be? Without a recipe however, how can I know what the final product will look like? How will I know what ingredients I'll need?

Going down this route without a recipe would result in a conversation along these lines:

**You:** "I need a wedding cake. It should have three tiers and I'll need it in three days."

**Me:** "Okay. I'll start baking it tomorrow."

I go to the shop to buy all the ingredients I think I'll need: eggs, flour, sugar, vanilla, chocolate...and whilst there, I see an elegant bride – and – groom cake topper. I think it will make a great addition to the cake, so decide to purchase it as well.

When I get home, I think to myself, "I wonder if anyone in the family has allergies." I decide to call and check but learn that you are away for a day on business.

I'll have to wait to continue. I finally manage to get hold of you and find out that your great Auntie Ethel is allergic to chocolate. I head back to the shop and decide to purchase some fruit instead. I start to build the layers of the cake. Everything is going well – except I'm now behind and starting to eat into my profits.

When you check in on my progress, you find that I decorated the cake with white icing. This is a problem because pink is the bride's favourite colour. I try to explain that pink icing will cost more and take additional time to pick up, but you insist that white simply won't do. In addition, you don't like my tacky bride and groom topper. However, it has given you an idea! Now, instead you want some writing on the top of cake.

Again, I explain that this was not part of the agreement.

You insist that your heart is now set on some romantic words in hot – pink lettering. I didn't realise how hard it would be to get the lettering right and find out that to be good at it, I need to attend a course. This adds even more time and expense to the project, which is now costing me more than what you had offered to pay. To make things worse the cake is now going to be late.

I have spent so much time going back and forth trying to make you happy, spending money beyond your budget, investing time that I don't have to spare. You are now left disappointed, still without a cake and I feel under appreciated and out – of – pocket. In fact, I've stopped answering your calls altogether because I can't face dealing with this anymore and don't know what to do.

This whole situation could have been avoided if I had acquired a few more details in the initial stages.

In the above scenario and from the comfort of reading this book, it's easy to say that I am at fault – but you are the one that would have to live with the fact that you didn't get your cake, at least not the one you wanted and when it was due.

I'm not trying to blame anyone here, but instead suggest that you have all the information you need so that when you are looking for that perfect cake, you at least know what to ask for.

If we change the scenario to website design, it is shocking how many developers do not have consultations with clients. It's also very scary how many people call themselves developers when really they are nothing more than glorified button pushers.

The consequences of clients not knowing what they want and subsequently hiring "developers" who don't know what questions to ask before the start of a project can create devastating results. In the past, I've had people literally begging me to help them out of a situation because they had no money due to a failed attempt with a previous developer and they now wanted me to pick up the pieces. For a while I did this. It's what contributed to my breakdown.

I wanted to prove that this was a real problem in the world and not just something that I had attributed to myself. I created a job description to test my theory and placed an advert on a well—known outsourcing website. It read as follows:

### Website Needed

I Need a website
It needs some pages
I want it to look really good
I need it in a week.

Would you believe that I received 53 responses within the first 24 hours? People from all over the world were telling me they could create my website. Prices ranged from $25 to $9500. I saw similar "copy and paste" responses over and over again from people desperate to try and win my work. How could they possibly know what I wanted? Maybe I would end up asking for a website that would dominate Facebook, or something with an algorithm similar to Google's. Would that have been included in the $25 proposal?

I think you get the point that unless you have some clarity and direction, it's most likely going to cause pain, lots of stress and you will probably lose some money in the process. You are likely tell all your friends just how unhelpful your new developer is and how you would not recommend them.

So how can you avoid this situation?

The first priority is to understand the importance of your plan. It is not meant to be set in stone. Instead, as previously described, it should be a strategic document that will allow you to brief your designer and developer so they can easily understand the fundamentals of what will be required.

Here's another analogy: Imagine that two people both own the same car and both vehicles have the exact same fault.

One car owner, Chelsea, is a qualified mechanic who has been working in the motor trade for the last fifteen years.

The other car owner, Dave, believes the most important feature of any car is an Italian leather interior. He admits that he knows nothing about how to check the oil or change a tyre.

They both visit the same garage.

Chelsea tells the mechanic exactly what she needs and is quoted a reasonable price for the parts and labour.

Dave, however, mentions how he knows nothing about cars and it is all very confusing. Could the garage just fix it? In the end, he is quoted over three times as much and is informed that there are several "other problems" that also need to be fixed.

Can you understand how this could happen with your website design? You owe it to yourself to ensure that you are informed and prepared when you seek a developer. Once you finish reading this book, you will possess the knowledge contained within all ten steps and will be prepared to create a plan that will lead to a successful website.

Each chapter of this book has been created around tasks that, when completed, act as stepping stones towards mastering your online presence

# CHAPTER 1
# STRATEGY

If you are anything like me, you can't wait to get started so let's dive in. This is without a doubt the most important chapter of the book, the most important part of your website build and the most important aspect to factor in the success or failure of your business.

You would be crazy to take health advice from someone who is obese and you would be just as mad to take financial advice from someone who has no money, so you better make sure that you take your website advice from someone who knows how to create successful websites.

I've built thousands of websites, some without any strategy, some with bad planning and some with an amazing plan. It's very easy looking back, to see which ones survived.

In fact, I learnt so much through my experience that I created an entire model around the acronym P.L.A.N. which stands for...

## Prepare

This is what the book encompasses and is critical for ensuring that you have a solid foundation. The introduction explained why you needed a strategy and the subsequent chapters will show you how to create one so that you are prepared to the best of your ability.

## List Build

Even before you have a website, you can start to create a database of people who are interested in your products or services, otherwise known as your "list." This is your most valuable asset in business and it will contain information on your potential and existing customers. Guard it with your life!

## Automate

A business can never be scalable if you're the lynchpin holding everything together. The more involved you become in the day to day operations, the less of a business owner you are. A better label would be an employee working for yourself. The outcome here is to create systems that take you out of your business to work ON it rather than IN it.

## Nurture

This is the magical elixir to business. What so many fail to realise is that when you nurture your customers, they become your raving fans. You literally create an army who happily market your products and services for free.

After spending the last two years writing this book, I can assure you that I considered the structure and order of the questions I will be asking very carefully. Whilst it may be tempting to gloss over them, I can testify from experience that those who ignore the first section ultimately bounce from project to project, from failure to failure.

With that said, there are key elements that you need to consider if you want to be successful online. Even though this book will explain and demonstrate what they are, the workbook that you can download from the link below will take you through each one step by step.

http://planyourwebsite.co.uk/workbook

So before we dive into your website, you first need to take a look at yourself. The reason for this is because your website is the window to your business and your business is a reflection of who you are as a person. We need to ascertain that you have clarity, certainty and are not operating from a place of negative emotions. Otherwise, embarking on this journey could cause you additional negative experiences.

# Who are you?

I can assure you that if you are focused on scarcity, lack, money, stress or anything negative, then it will transfer into what you create and you will, by virtue, attract the very thing that you are trying to avoid.

You may ask what this has got to do with a website. That would be a great question.

You are the person who runs your business. Who you are and what you focus on determine how your business is shaped. As I mentioned, your website is the window to that business. So if you are not in alignment with your business, then your website will show this and will result in either limited traffic and sales — or worse, poor quality traffic and customers who you don't want, distracting you from your goals.

Before you consider the following, I would take a few deep breaths and find quiet sanctuary where you can meditate on your thoughts to ensure that you find the best answers possible. Sometimes putting on your favourite music before starting this process can help to clear your mind. Dancing or just moving around can also help to become more creative.

Are you currently in a positive mindset? If no, then get there before you continue reading! We first need to consider who you are, what your core values are and what you are passionate about. This will play a huge part when things become difficult — which I promise, they will. We all face challenges. It's a sign of being alive. Even when successful, you will still experience them. It's just that they will just be different. The trick is to always be bigger than the problems that you face. That way you can see over them and not become engulfed in a struggle.

Having a clear purpose will help drive you forward when things get tough and knowing what makes you passionate will push you through the challenging times. It separates those who just want to throw up a quick and cheap website from someone who wants to make a real difference in the world. How much time you spend preparing will determine the quality of what you produce.

When potential clients come to me asking for a great website, built overnight with no budget, I refer them to the diagram below. I think it really explains the choice that many face when starting out. If you could only pick two of the three main circles, which would they be?

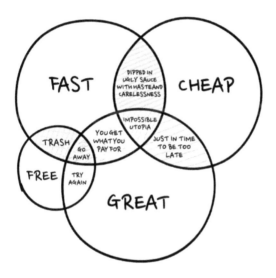

Early on, it is also important to create your personal bio and your elevator pitch that you can use proudly to promote yourself. Your pitch is a carefully crafted answer to the question "So, what do you do?" Note I asked what YOU do, not what your business does. This is important because people do not buy from a business, they buy from a person. For this reason, it makes sense that you show a human element to what you are about to create. The more you position yourself as the expert, the more you will attract the clients that you want to work with and those who will help you realize your goal

# What is your business?

Now that we have identified who you are, we need to take a look at your business, which at its core, is simply a way of adding value. In other words, somebody will have a problem and your business will offer a solution, the value is taking the person from the problem to the solution. It's this distance between the before and after which impacts how much you can charge.

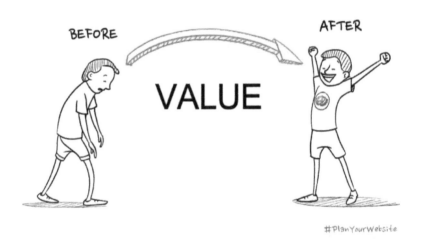

#PlanYourWebsite

In essence, the sole purpose of a business is to generate income. You may have your own agenda, ideas and beliefs (and that's why we started by looking at yourself) but the business needs to survive and for that it needs to be profitable.

For it to create profit, you need to add value, so a great place to start here is to consider how your business will achieve this. I often find that not having clarity here becomes the ideal breeding ground for procrastination. So many entrepreneurs and start—ups fail to identify the outcome of their business or they spend an eternity going round in circles. It is important to get something out at this stage that is 80% of what you want and then you can revisit it later.

*"Any fool can make something complicated. It takes a genius to make it simple."* ~ Woody Guthrie

The best way to start here is by looking at your company's mission statement. This, in its most simplistic terms, is one paragraph that sums up what your business does. By identifying this, it will become your moral compass, guiding you through challenging times because when you know your outcome, you can strive towards it no matter what gets thrown in your way. This is the one thing in your business that should not change unless given great and careful consideration about the effect it could have. This declaration should underpin everything that you do and drive the decisions throughout. It is the ultimate purpose of the business so take some time and make it outstanding.

Once you have your mission statement, you can elaborate to create your company bio. This is similar to your personal bio but should focus on what problems you are going to fix as a business, what the core values of the business are, the ethics and foundations you will build upon and anything that will ensure the survival of your business venture.

As you write your company bio, it makes sense to do your research and look at your competition. See what they are doing. If possible, purchase their products and services and see how they interact with you as a customer. Identify areas of weakness and focus on how you can improve on what is currently being offered.

Also, you should find out if there is a demand for what you're offering, if there's actually a marketplace for you. Or do you need to create one?

A really important concept to consider here would be your top three USVP's. This stands for "Unique Selling Value Proposition," similar in marketing terms to the USP but I've added V because it's all about the value that you add. Some like to call this your superpower. It's the key benefit that will set you apart and make you better than everyone else. Why will people come to you? Trust you? Use your products and services? Ultimately, why will people buy from you rather than a competitor? You need to understand and identify this as it will drive what you do and why you are doing it.

A great example of this is the shoe company called TOMS shoes. They sell comfy and inexpensive footwear that alone isn't really enough to make them stand out in the shoe business. However, their USVP is that for every pair you purchase, they donate a new pair to a child in need. It's this added value that helps them stand out in a crowded marketplace.

One of the main reasons we need to know how you are different is because it will come out in the content of the website, in the way you communicate, in your marketing style, and in the way you interact with your clients.

# Who is your Target Audience?

This question is so important. Take serious time to consider this question because if you get it wrong or gloss over it, then you may end up looking for business in the wrong places and not attracting anyone at all. Or worse, you could end up attracting the wrong quality of client into your business and spend countless hours and unnecessary energy dealing with them.

If you approach business with the attitude that you are going to promote to everyone then you will undoubtedly struggle. There is a saying that if you market to everyone then you're selling to no one. You need to be specific because it is in that specificity that you will identify a certain audience- and once you have engaged them, others will follow.

Perry Marshall, a world—class expert in marketing, stated that 80% of your revenue will come from 20% of your customers. As a result, it makes sense early on to identify who your target audience is.

Another word for this group of people is a "niche."

Some of the most successful people take this a step further and create what is known in the industry as a "super niche," which is simply a very specific group of people with a targeted interest or challenge.

An example of this could be golf. Lots of people want to learn how to play and it's easy to imagine a school that gives golf lessons to every type of golfer: kids, adults etc. Here, the niche is just "golf lessons." The school generally helps everyone.

Let's dive a little deeper. There are professional golfers that compete in tournaments. Often they have a coach who helps them to improve their game. These people are not interested in a school that helps everyone. They are looking for something more specific. These people would be more interested in being coached by someone who specialises in key areas like helping golfers drive the ball further than anyone else. That is a "super niche." It's a very specific part of a niche and by finding the problem (people who want help improving their driving) you can position yourself as an authority figure.

People, products, services and brands are typically noticed because they stand out. They target a specific group of people and by being the best they become world class at dealing with just one thing. You don't always remember someone when they are vague or blend in.

A great example of a brand standing out is Virgin. When you consider them as an airline, they have a very different message to British Airways. As a result, they have a different target audience and this creates different marketing campaigns although both for the same industry. Even budget airlines like Ryanair have a specific target audience that they attract.

Without a target audience, you can waste countless marketing budgets, time and energy trying to convince people that you are the best solution for them. Normally you end up attracting the clients you don't want because business is about survival after all, and you still need to make money. I have seen it happen and it can stop you moving forward with your vision.

*"If you don't have the clients you want, it's because you're too busy attracting the ones you already have." ~ Allison Rapp*

So...

The big question here should be, "How do I identify who my ideal target audience is?"

It's a great question and one that can be answered by creating a "customer avatar."

An avatar is a specific description of a fictitious character who you would consider your ideal client, complete with backstory, profile picture, habits and traits. You should emotionally connect with your avatar and step into their world describing what you see, how you feel and what you think in as much detail as possible.

These are some areas to start considering but this is not a definitive list. Also, depending on the problem you solve, some of these questions may or may not be relevant to you. Generally speaking, the more relevant questions you ask, the better.

Here are a few things to consider: You need to know if they are male or female; whether they are more laid back or if they're blunt; what good and bad habits they have; what makes them laugh or get angry; what their ambitions are; what stops them moving forward in their lives; how you can inspire them to take action; what their financial situation is; where they go to socialise and how they like to spend free time.

Depending on your business, you may also want to explore their family life — where and how they grew up, what their parents are like, whether or not they have a partner now, if they are married, and what their intimate relationships are like.

These questions will help you to imagine a very detailed person who you can communicate to. For example, you would probably talk differently to a teenager than to an old aged pensioner. The backstory for your customer avatar creates an emotional connection so that you can resonate with them in your content and build rapport. It's a great way to stand out.

There are more purposes to a customer avatar than just identifying your target audience. When you understand the habits of your market, you can get a much better idea of patterns and then use this information to know when the ideal times to communicate and best locations to market to them are.

I have many customer avatars in different areas of my business that have not only shaped how I market my products but also how I create them. Yes, even this book had three customer avatars to help me identify my message to my ideal reader. You can check them out in the workbook.

I based them loosely on several previous clients, some good and some bad. This allowed me to identify with what I wanted myself as an ideal customer in my business.

It's common for web designers to leave the customer avatar step out of the process when they make a website for someone — and even very successful entrepreneurs can have this happen.

A great example of this was a client of mine. He is a two – time Olympic champion, motivational speaker, author and world – renowned health expert. You can tell just by looking at him how much he works out and looks after himself. He has a range of physical and digital products as well as supplements that he successfully sells from his website. When I met him, he was often speaking at events where the room would be packed out and he would sell so many products-but his website sales were not doing nearly as well.

I took a look at his website analytics and the first thing that struck me was the majority of his audience were female. They were arriving at a website that had a black background and big bold fonts. Now this may not seem like much, but combined with the content on his website, it became apparent why he was losing sales online. Most of his problem was because he had not identified his target audience with his previous website designer, and they had built something that didn't speak to his fans.

One of the biggest challenges I recognise when people approach me is when they say "I need a website!"

I often start this dialogue with "Tell me what you want?" and this in most cases this leads to them explaining all the things that they want, for them. Often I have to say the website is not for them. It's for their target audience. After all, these will be the people using the site and spending most of the time on it. They will be the ones that buy from you, so it's important to establish trust as soon as possible and to ensure that your brand identity and message resonate with them. Once you have rapport, they will be more confident that they are in the right place and you are the right person for them to do business with.

We go over this in a lot more detail in the workbook section called 'How to Build a Customer Avatar.'

# What is your Exit Strategy?

Most of the time when I talk to people about having an exit strategy before even having started their business, they think I'm crazy. I mean, why would you consider exiting your business when you are only just thinking about setting it up?

This might not make sense but trust me when I tell you that one day, you WILL exit your business.

It might be on a plane heading for a remote private island or the worst—case scenario, in a coffin, but one day, you will exit your business. It is this reason that makes it so important to start setting yourself up now so that you can one day exit your business. I'm not talking as extreme as the plane or coffin examples, but things happen in life. You may get bored. You may get an irresistible offer to sell or you may get sick. Whatever the reason, you should have the ability to replace yourself within the business and it can be achieved without the stress when you plan your exit from the start.

By thinking about automated systems and standard operating procedures, you can enable other people to come into the business and continue to run it in your absence. This also gives you more flexibility to take a step back from the day to day operations so that you can work ON your business and not IN it.

Back in 2010, I created a t—shirt printing business and had just purchased some machinery to get started. About a week after doing this, I was looking online and found the exact same machine that I had purchased for less than 50% of what I had just paid. My initial thought was to buy this machine and sell it for more so I could make a quick profit. However, after speaking to the lady that owned it, I found she was selling her entire business. I brought external investors on board to fund the purchase and not only did we get that machine, several others, an abundance of stock, and hundreds of new clients, but we also inherited a fantastic relationship with her offshore manufacturer.

Great news for us — but why did she sell it?

The reason I share this story is because she had a profitable business and things were going great. Then, due to unforeseen health issues, she was in hospital and unable to work for almost six months. Having fourteen staff with no direction meant that things slowly ground to a halt. By the time she was well enough to continue, she decided it was too much for her to revive the business and decided to sell what was left.

Imagine, in that scenario, if she had the automated systems or procedures in place for her business to continue to operate in her absence. I remember one phone call. It was heart—breaking to listen to the story of how she spent 40 years of her life building up this business. Her reputation within her industry preceded her. Her life, her friends and her income were all centered around her business but after surgery she felt too weak to pick up the pieces of the business. In addition to this, she was also on the verge of a breakthrough that was about to change part of her industry and the lives of thousands of children around the country. This dream crumbled with the business. The only comfort that she got from selling was to know that rather than dismantle everything, it would be kept together to give someone else the opportunity to create something like she once did.

Considering your exit strategy does not mean that you are planning to leave right now, but it will force you to create systems that do not require you to be involved. This can be hard to deal with at first, especially if you have an ego to contend with. It will however, serve you better when realising that your business can survive without you and your focus is on more than just the day to day operations.

What is your exit strategy?

This question gets you to start looking at your business from a different perspective.

Typical developers won't ask you this question because realistically, your business is not their primary concern. They are not specifically interested in you or your future. They just want to build your website and they just want to get paid.

I'm looking deeper at you, what you want and how you're going to set yourself apart, so that you can have the life that you want as opposed to a life that you may have. To do that, you need to ask this question.

And don't worry. You may not have all the answers now. That's ok. Not knowing should not stop you. Just keep your exit strategy in mind as you grow.

# What is your Timeframe?

As with any good plan, you need to have an idea of how long things will take and allow a certain buffer for unforeseen circumstances.

The main question to ask first is, "When do you want to launch?"

I often tell people to set a date and make sure it is in the diary. This becomes the date you launch your website. The rest of the process is simply reverse engineering to ensure all the pieces are in place.

Give yourself a fighting chance. Tomorrow is not very realistic. With that in mind, I have launched websites within a day before so it is possible, you just need to appreciate that it's not going to be the best it can be.

Seriously consider when you want to launch. It's worth noting that a launch typically has three phases:

- the pre – launch
- the launch
- the post – launch

Whilst choosing your launch date, ask yourself if anything is going on around that time. Are there any holidays, national or global events, industry – specific or competitor promotions that could affect what you are doing?

Also, consider the timing in relation to your target audience. You don't want to launch a website selling Valentine's Day cards just after the event or start to sell winter clothes at the start of summer.

If you were going to launch a website that sold stationery and you specifically decided to niche into the market of schools, then you might consider launching during the school holidays. You might consider running a campaign from the middle to just after they return so that you can attract the keen, organised people that want to be ready and the last minute rushers who are trying to get things together.

If you're a public speaker and you're planning a speaking event but your audience are going to be at a different event listening to another speaker on the day you launch, it could affect sales. I appreciate that you can't prepare for every eventuality but having an idea helps. Also consider things like location. If you booked a hotel to hold your conference and a national event like the World Cup were happening nearby, people might find it challenging to get to you. It's all about the advance thinking and planning around things that could be avoided to give everyone the best experience.

On the flip side, consider when you do launch there may be something in the news or trending on social media. It may be possible to piggyback on this story to get some additional exposure that you wouldn't otherwise receive.

Apple are a great example when they are about to launch a new model iPhone. Especially if you are selling iPhone cases, you may want to put the launch of your company around a launch of the new Apple iPhone, so when a customer gets their new iPhone, they can get their new case. You can ride the wave from an industry trend to help increase initial sales.

As mentioned earlier, another great benefit of planning your launch date is giving you the ability to create your "pre—launch."

Your pre—launch is where you will create excitement and start to generate a buzz around what you are creating. This is the perfect opportunity to create a series of marketing campaigns. You only have to look at Apple and the way they unveil a new product to understand how effective this can be.

It's also a perfect time to start building your list of interested people so that when you launch, you can hit the ground running. Even before you have a website, you can create a holding page that has the ability to collect names and email addresses so that you can inform them when you launch. There could also be an incentive for these people because they are early adopters and if you nurture them right, they will soon become brand ambassadors and raving fans.

As you start to build rapport with your target audience by positioning yourself in their awareness, you will build a level of trust. When you come to launch, people will already feel like they know you and have experienced part of your journey with you and will be able to relate to your message in a way that impacts them to make the decision to invest in your product or services.

You would be amazed how many people fail to plan a pre-launch strategy and when they launch just rely on a post on social media and telling a few friends and family members about the new website. There is nothing worse than only the site owner and developer knowing it exists. It's like putting a fountain in the middle of a barren desert. Sure, people who stumble upon it will be grateful- but it's never going to get the attention it would if placed in a city centre.

Finally, setting a launch date is really important so you can understand what you need to do in terms of preparation, design and build and marketing. Simple Square did a really good job of creating this diagram that shows the overall process of building a successful website and some things that you need to consider. How long is it going to take you to get your content ready? What about your design? The systems? The testing?

Once you know what your launch date is, you can reverse engineer what needs to be done within that time frame to get you where you need to be.

# A Website Designed
MILESTONES, INVOLVEMENT, IMPORTANCE & TIMELINE

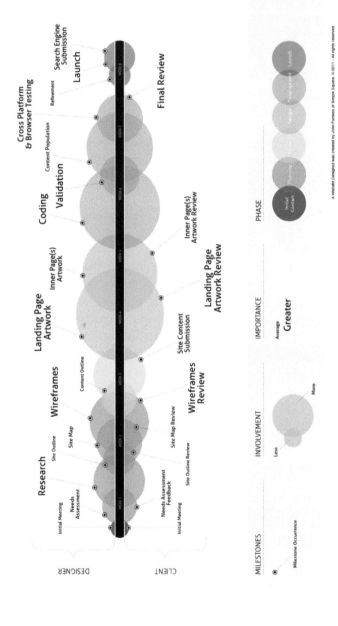

DESIGNER

CLIENT

Research

Initial Meeting
Needs Assessment
Site Outline
Site Map

Wireframes

Content Outline

Landing Page Artwork

Inner Page(s) Artwork

Coding

Content Population
Validation

Cross Platform & Browser Testing
Refinement

Launch

Search Engine Submission

Final Review

Initial Meeting
Needs Assessment Feedback
Site Outline Review
Site Map Review

Wireframes Review

Site Content Submission

Landing Page Artwork Review

Inner Page(s) Artwork Review

WEEK 1  WEEK 2  WEEK 3  WEEK 4  WEEK 5  WEEK 6  WEEK 7  WEEK 8

MILESTONES
Milestone Occurrence

INVOLVEMENT
Less
More

IMPORTANCE
Average
Greater

PHASE
Initial Contact
Planning
Design
Development
Launch

30

# What is your Budget?

One of the more taboo questions to be asked in the early stages is the one that revolves around money. Depending on your mindset, generally speaking, you will be divided into two categories of people: Those looking for a free solution and those willing to pay for it. Neither is right or wrong. They just require different approaches. What you sometimes save in money can cost more in time and energy. (Although this is not always the case as sometimes good things can cost less.) It's about doing your due diligence and making the best decision you can, at that moment in time.

It astounds me how many people when asked what their budget is reply, "I'm not sure, I don't really have one."

The reason people don't know their budget is because they don't know what they need, so they can't judge what to spend.

In 2010, the UK government had a website created which cost in excess of £105,000,000. (That's not a typo.) Yes that's £35 million a year for three years. After the three years, it was deemed that the website didn't work and so it was closed down. CLOSED DOWN. They spent £105 million and the website didn't work so they shut it down. The government were so used to working with old school corporate giants that had not embraced new technology. Had they taken the time to plan their website, it could have saved them at least 80% of the budget. Hindsight, eh? The moral of this story is that it's not about throwing money at a problem, it's about investing the right amount of money into the best solution for it.

So I ask you. Do you have a budget equal to the UK Government?

I assume the answer is no. The good news is now we know what is too high for your budget.

The BBC reported how the UK National Health Service spent £21 million on their website, NHS Choices. Unlike the aforementioned, this was more of a success, attracting on average 40 million unique visitors a month.

So my next question is, do you have a budget equal to the NHS?

I'm going to assume the answer is still no.

There is no right or wrong budget. You just need a number that resonates with you. It should not be everything and it should not be zero. It needs to be a figure that you can use to invest in products and services that will assist you in building your successful online presence. There is no point planning for a system that will cost you £300 a month to maintain if your total budget is only £50. This question is designed to move you towards your outcome in a realistic way.

What you don't spend in budget for strategy, design and development at the start you will most likely spend in troubleshooting, hacking systems together or therapy bills later on. I urge you to start lowering the number from the previous examples to a more realistic figure until you can once again breathe at the thought of investing in your business.

Notice how I used the word "investing," because I do not consider the cost of a website to be an "expense." I consider it to be an investment. You want to achieve a positive ROI (return on investment) and I do not understand why anyone would create a website that has the ability to reach a global audience 24 hours a day, 7 days a week 365 days a year if they were not intending to maximize its potential to do this.

When we look deeper into a budget, it can be broken down into two core elements.

## One—Off Payments

The one—off payments would be relevant to areas such as strategy, design, development, initial content writing, etc. Once you have paid for them, you own them and no longer have to pay for their upkeep (unless you want additional work in the future).

## Recurring Costs

These are your monthly and annual costs that are required to both run and maintain your website and the systems that you use. (Note: I am not referring to the many online template systems that you can use which offer you a website for a monthly fee. You do not own these websites and if the service changes its terms and conditions or closes, your business will ultimately disappear with the provider. So, you should ensure that you own and can use your website independently of any third party template providers.)

To have a website you own requires at the minimum three things. I like to use an analogy of a house to explain this better.

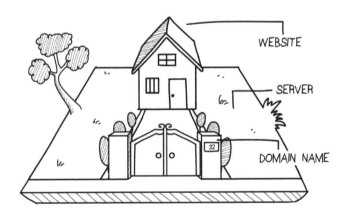

Now, imagine your house is your website (containing all the files and folders), the land is your server and your door number is your domain name so people can find you. You need all three and they all work together.

Your domain name has an annual cost attached to it payable to the registration company (registrar). The price will depend on the company you use and also the extension of that domain. For example, names ending in .com generally cost more than .co.uk.

Once you have your domain, you need to consider hosting for your website. Every website needs a computer to store the files. I'm not talking about your home computer, but a dedicated server that is designed specifically to host websites, which is what gives us the name "hosting."

Businesses rent out space on their servers to host your website files and depending on who you use and what you pay, there are variations in the quality of system and the level of support that you receive. Cheaper is not always the best option here, although people often don't realise that until they are faced with the problems that arise from a cheap hosting provider.

I have lost count how many times I have seen a post on social media asking "What is the best hosting provider to use?" It's followed by an onslaught of suggestions from people who mean well but don't have a clue what they are talking about. What may work for one person won't always work for another and it makes sense to look at what you need both now and in the future before you consider what provider you should use.

Here is a list of some typical examples of ongoing costs that you may incur. This is not a definitive list. It's more something to give you an idea. Don't worry about the terminology, we cover many of these things later in Chapter 7.

- Domain Name
- SSL Certificate
- Hosting
- Marketing Content
- Email Accounts
- Tracking Software
- Website Maintenance
- Third Party Plugins
- E – Commerce
- Payment Gateways
- Book Keeping Software
- Email Auto responders

Technology is moving fast. One prominent change that we have witnessed in recent years is software companies leaning towards the model known as software as a service (SAAS). This model changes the previous one – time licence fee for a product into a recurring cost. Rather than you purchasing a license and downloading the software onto your system, you would instead connect to the internet and use a version they manage and maintain. This allows greater support from the software company in terms of updates, bug testing and maintenance but it does often incur monthly or annual fees. Generally, unless you build something or download and maintain it yourself, you will have to consider paying a recurring fee for the privilege of logging in and using it.

A great example of this is Google. You can get a free personal email address to use but if you want to create a business one linked to your domain name, then you have to pay them a monthly fee. They maintain the email servers in terms of security, performance, hardware and software updates whilst you just log into your account and use their service.

It's worth mentioning at this point that some of the best software on the market today is "open source." Generally, open source refers to a computer program in which the source code is available to the general public for use and/or modification from its original design. Open – source code is meant to be a collaborative effort, where programmers improve upon the source code and share the changes within the community. The best example of open source is the content management system called WordPress. Currently running 30% of websites on the internet, it has become the world's leading platform and can be downloaded and used for free under a general public licence.

Whilst "free" can be good, it can also have its limitations, specifically regarding the support provided. Businesses delivering free services are normally much less inclined to spend time offering support when compared to services which charge a premium. I've seen exceptions to this when the free service is a loss leader into something bigger but in general, free does not come without a price tag.

The final thing I would recommend in this section is your marketing budget. It's a common mistake to assume that once you build it they will come. A website is only successful if people find it. Whilst there are many organic ways to build traffic, they can take time. You should offset for marketing and promotional material that can be used to position yourself. Social media will only take you so far and your friends and family will embrace you for a while but ultimately you need to be getting your message in front of your target audience. The quickest and most effective way to do that during and just after a launch is to put a budget aside for advertising costs.

Remember that your website is the window to your business. It is your responsibility to make it look as appealing as possible so that customers will eventually purchase from you.

# What is Your Online Identity?

Also known as IID or "internet identity," your online presence is represented by two things: you as a person and the brand of your business.

Often people have challenges separating the two but just consider how some of the most influential entrepreneurs in the world have two identities. Richard Branson is known for his personality but also for Virgin. Bill Gates is also known for Microsoft, Steve Jobs for Apple and Mark Zuckerberg for Facebook.

When people recognise they need a website, they sometime miss other aspects that contribute to the overall picture- things like email correspondence, social media profiles, forum and blog signatures. It's a combination of all these elements that contributes towards your online identity and that of your business, which should always be kept separate from your personal identity. Remember your exit strategy?

It was so tough to find the right place for this section. I would say at least a week was spent banging my head against the table before making a decision. It's important you know this information and I wanted to share it before talking about the budget but decided the previous sections will help you make a better informed decision about your online identity.

It's also important to understand that I could write another book entirely around this subject. It was difficult to ensure that I give you the key information without overwhelming you or losing sight of the outcome- so please know that even though this information is important, it's only an introduction to what is a much larger concept.

*"A rose by any other name would smell as sweet." ~ William Shakespeare, Romeo and Juliet*

Whilst this may be true for Romeo and Juliet, it's not the same for your online identity. You simply cannot afford to cut corners when it comes to choosing such an important aspect of your business. Your name is how you will be perceived by the world and to avoid future pain you should really take time to consider how best to appear in the eyes of your target audience.

A saying I love and often recite is "Be the brand you want to see in the world." This was introduced to me by the owners of How to Build a Brand. I find it very interesting because many business owners create an image in the present and do not consider where they will be in the future. Sometimes people think they are too small to have a brand. It's a misconception because everybody, from the moment they start a business, has a brand. This is covered in more detail later in the book.

If you are not growing, you're dying. So it makes sense when creating a new business to focus on growth. As you become more established and secure, you will undoubtedly start to view things in a different light. Therefore, I would urge you to consider when thinking about your brand and online identity to not look at where you are when you start, but where you are going. I want you to step into the future and claim your identity now so you can embody the business you want to become and strive towards it with power, passion and clarity.

For the purpose of simplicity, I've divided this section into two main components, domain names and social media usernames.

# Domain Names

Firstly, what is a domain name? In it's most simplistic term it is a string of text used to identify your website. It can be referred to as a URL and often looks like this

www.planyourwebsite.co.uk

A domain name will start with http:// or if it is secure https:// (the secure version requires an SSL certificate and can be identified with a green padlock from the browser).

Some people think that a domain name must start with www. but this is not true. Many larger websites use subdomains to break up content and this replaces the initial www. that you traditionally see on websites. Many companies would use this for support or membership areas.

Below is an example of a full domain name with all the working parts.

Whilst most people try to purchase a domain name as close to the name of their business, it's not always possible or good sense. When considering your domain name, you need to be aware of two main things: how it is perceived by search engines and how it is perceived by people.

A domain might be great for search engines but it might not be memorable or easy to write down. Also, a domain that is short and snappy is not always going to give you the organic traffic that is vital to grow your business. A healthy balance is recommended and in some cases, multiple domain names could provide a better solution.

You will find that most of the premium domain names are already occupied– if not by a business, then often by domain squatters who purchase them in bulk to be sold later for profit. Some people also buy domain names not because they are needed, but simply to stop competition from using them.

Whatever the reason, it can become very overwhelming and frustrating trying to find your perfect domain name. Some companies have disregarded all the advice and created new ways in order to combat this growing challenge. Companies have even created new words like Spotify or Bitly. Be prepared though if you are going to choose something that is unfamiliar or a new concept, then you will require a strong marketing campaign and budget to push the awareness to market.

So why do you need a domain name?

We have already mentioned that search engines trawl the internet indexing all the domains into a directory. The most popular of these being Google, Bing and Yahoo. Here are some other reasons to establish your own professional domain name:

- Gain exposure for your website
- Increase your brand awareness
- Protect copyrights and trademarks
- Block competitors from stealing potential customers
- Establish a reputable presence online
- Allow you to create a professional email address
- Make it easier for people to find you

There are a few things to consider when looking for your domain name.

## How it sounds

It should roll off the tongue, be ideally as close to two syllables as possible and be something that's not going to be mistaken for anything else when it is pronounced.

Imagine trying to say the following www.this-is-mynew-domain-name.com now imagine trying to explain it to someone so they can type it.

## How is it remembered

The best way to test a potential domain name is to mention it to someone. Change the conversation and check back in five minutes to see if they remembered it. A simple and catchy name will be easier to remember than one you have to explain to people.

## How it looks and types

Once you have an idea you should write it down. How does it look? Remember to avoid special characters and underscores (because website links are always underlined as standard so it won't be seen). Your domain name should be easy to type, easy to spell and easy to read. Short and sweet is the key so keep away from those long and complicated names. Remember this will also become a big part of your email address so choose carefully and consider the people who have to type it in when they want to communicate with you.

Here are some examples of how things appear differently:

Experts Exchange is a knowledge base where programmers can exchange advice and views @
www.ExpertSexChange.com
www.ExpertsExchange.com

Looking for a pen? Look no further than Pen Island @
www.PenisLand.net
www.PenIsland.net

The designers at Speed of Art await you on their website @
www.SpeedoFart.com
www.SpeedOfArt.com

## Pre—Purchase Checks

Make sure that before you purchase a domain it's clean as this
can cause you great trouble if your build your site around a
domain that has a shady past. Just run a quick check if a
domain was once used for bad practice. It could be blocked or
listed on multiple databases as malicious.

**Site age:** If it's a used domain, first visit a website called "The
Wayback Machine." Make sure there aren't any previous
associations with pornography, hate, violence or piracy. If
there are, it's best to avoid the domain as there may still be
references online.

**Blacklists check:** Take a moment to check if the domain name
has been blacklisted in the past. You can use search engines to
find services that will do this for free.

**URL length:** On the other end of relevancy is the issue of being
too specific. Don't get too long and detailed. You can always
get more specific as you go deeper into subdomains. Shorter
domain names are easier to remember– and type!

**Potential for legal conflict:** Be aware of trademarks and
copyrights belonging to other entities. While a URL like
www.wordpressdeveloper.com might be accurate to your
web design business, it violates a trademark owned by
WordPress that prohibits using their name in domain names.
If something comes up that seems like a potential conflict, it
most likely is.

**Top—level domain:** Choose the right top—level domain
(.com, .net, .org, .info, and so on). Businesses should always
consider using .com because it's still the industry standard
and the most widely recognised. Whilst there is nothing

wrong with using country—specific domains, they are not perceived as being as "professional" as .com.

The .org domain is still perceived as non—profit or for charitable purposes and it is used by many groups or organisations. Additional country specific .org domains have been introduced such as .org.uk which are still popular but add a little extra into the name so it is best to stick with the original unless you are really stuck.

Top—level domains like .info and .biz are often associated, rightly or wrongly, with spammers and a top—level domain can have an impact on your overall search engine optimisation. For example, a link to your website from a .edu or .gov website is considered more prestigious than one from a .com or a .biz website.

**Keyword research:** Does the domain use popular and focused keywords? Make sure the domain and its associated URLs will be conducive to search engine visibility.

### Cost of a Domain Name
Typically, the two most popular UK domain names are .co.uk and .com

A .co.uk domain name right now will cost in the region of between £5—10 whilst a .com domain will cost between £10—15 per annum. You can purchase domain names for one year at a time but I would always recommend a minimum two year lease. It acts as a subconscious driving force for success.

# Social Media Usernames
Once you find your domain name, you are halfway there, although you still need to ensure that you can create usernames on the popular social media websites. Here, people often stick to the four main players which are Facebook, Twitter, LinkedIn and YouTube.

I would say that regardless of your industry, it makes sense to have accounts with these and then consider not which platforms you are using, but which platforms your target audience are using.

If you are a musician looking to create a website based on music, then it would benefit you to have accounts with SoundCloud, Myspace or Spotify. If you are a photographer looking to get your images into the world, then consider Instagram, Pinterest and Flickr to name a few.

I always recommend that you first create a profile picture that can be represented across all platforms. You should have both a personal profile image of yourself and a square logo that represents your brand. You also need a cover image. Some social media sites have rules around these so please check before creating them with too many words, self—promotion, etc.

Finally, have a well written bio about your business or yourself that others can read and relate to. Don't forget to include your domain name so that people can find your website if they are interested in learning more.

Once you have this information, it's a simple process of listing out all the platforms that you will use and creating accounts for them. I personally have an email folder specifically for any social media updates so my inbox does not get overwhelmed with updates.

I recommend a great free service to check the availability of all social media websites at once. Find out more in the workbook.

One final point is to consider that Twitter limits the characters of a username to fifteen, so start there to find a suitable name and then check the other platforms. Ideally, you want to create the same username for all your social media profiles so that others can find you with ease.

That's the end of the first chapter. How do you feel?

This first chapter was all about the strategy. The remainder of the book is about the different elements that will make up your overall strategy. By completing this section, you have "eaten the frog." (If you are unaware of the saying, then please check out Brian Tracy's book, *Eat That Frog!* which explains about doing the hardest part first.) Subsequent chapters of this book will be easier for some but nothing should be as difficult as what you have just been through.

# CHAPTER 2
# THE CUSTOMER JOURNEY

The previous chapter was the foundation for everything you are about to read. It was designed to help you gain clarity around yourself and your business so we can move forward with certainty. I would highly recommend that you read this book fully and then reference back when completing your workbook as your perspective may shift.

It is my belief that this chapter is the catalyst which gives you the ability to make your online presence "successful." The content was only realised by chance when a string of events took me on an adventure that would change my life forever. After all, the most memorable part of life is the journey we take, not the destination. (Remember this when mapping the journey of your customers to your product or service!)

In January 2015, I posted a message on Facebook asking for help getting me to America. It was the first time and I was only going to surprise a girl I'd never met for Valentine's Day. The thread had hundreds of comments from people with ideas ranging from contacting the airline for a PR stunt to wrapping myself up as a parcel. The winner came from a good friend, Marc P Summers who was sponsoring an event in San Diego the following month. He agreed to pay for my flight and accommodation if I helped him during the event.

It was during this time at the Traffic & Conversion Summit, North America's largest internet marketing event that I got to meet the experts who I had been following online for the previous two years. Legends in their own right and celebrities in their industries, I was honoured to be rubbing shoulders with them. One person I had the pleasure of spending time with was Russell Brunson, a successful internet marketer from Boise, Idaho who in just one of his online businesses was bringing in almost $20,000 a day! I had been paying close attention to Russell for some time because he was fast establishing himself as the leading authority regarding sales funnels and was bold enough at one point to state that you do not need a website, you need a sales funnel.

When I first met Russell, I told him how I both loved and hated him simultaneously. Loved because he had simplified the sales funnel process and explained it in a way that would allow me to re — evaluate my entire business and that of my clients. Hated because armed with this new information, I needed to rewrite my entire book. For me, the two years it took to publish were due to this missing chapter. At the time however, I couldn't put my finger on exactly what "it" was. You may also find that the missing "something" on your website could well be the customer journey.

When people build a website, it's often done to serve a purpose, except most do not know what the purpose is. Some say that they want to promote themselves, some just want a presence online to appear more professional. Only a few who understand the power in technology want it to help them build a list and sell their products or services. As I mentioned in the first chapter, when we started to identify your business, its sole purpose is survival. It achieves that by making profit and the only way a business can make a profit ethically is to sell something of value.

A website has the capability to be online 24 hours a day, 7 days a week 365 days a year so it makes sense to automate as much of it as possible. The trick with systems is ensuring you do not lose the personal touch with your audience. The idea behind the sales funnel is to map out a section of your customer's journey which creates profit in your business.

The diagram below gives you a very basic overview of how a basic customer journey map might look.

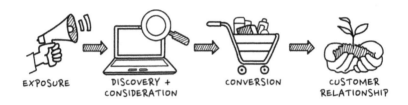

EXPOSURE          DISCOVERY +          CONVERSION          CUSTOMER
                  CONSIDERATION                            RELATIONSHIP

The best way to understand what your customers need and how you are going to provide this value is to first, ask yourself the following questions: "What is the outcome for the person who has landed on my website? Would buying a specific physical product benefit them? Would joining an online membership help them move closer to their goal? Do they need to schedule time with me?"

By looking at similar questions relevant to your business, you can start to understand what you will create as an "opt in gift," an "initial product," your "core offer" and any "upsells" that will add additional value at the time of purchase. The focus must always remain on the outcome of your audience. After all, they are the ones who pay your wages.

People can be introduced to your business via social media, word of mouth, search engines, paid advertising, etc. All of these sources of referrals are known as "traffic." While the funnel may change, the outcome is always the same: to convert traffic into profit by providing massive value.

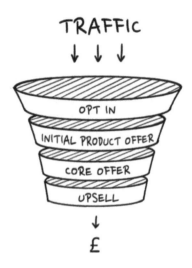

## The Opt In

The first question we need to ask when people find us online is "What happens if they leave?" Let's imagine your new visitor gets distracted and leaves your website without purchasing anything. How do you even know they were there in the first place? It makes sense to obtain contact information so if they click away, you can continue a conversation with them. An opt—in leads to this by allowing visitors to knowingly subscribe to a list so you can communicate by sending them relevant information.

Since the start of the internet, email has always ruled as a preferred choice of communication and even with social media and other platforms, email continues to dominate. That is not to say that things won't change in the future, but for now it's still the best way to contact your audience. At the time of writing this book, "push notifications" are becoming a very valuable marketing method. Apps are transitioning into the best form of communication due to more people using mobile devices than ever before.

Regardless of how you build your list, you should always consider this very important advice. Third party applications like social media, instant messengers and SAAS products are NOT the best way to store your clients' contact information. When you rely on an external entity to store your list, you are effectively putting your business's most valuable asset into someone else's control. If you are going to use them, please make sure you have the ability to export regular backups.

Imagine creating a group for your business on a social media platform. Let's say you attract a few thousand members and communicate with them by posting on the group and sending messages. The platform then decides to change its terms and conditions and for this example, your group name now causes a conflict. You log in one day but can't find your group, only a few scattered messages here and there. It slowly dawns your group has gone, along with everyone who was a member. (This happens all the time. Just last week, I saw a very active group with over 40,000 members closed– rightly so for trademark infringement.) My point being, if you rely on a third party platform to control your list then you have no long term business, and you have no list. One of the most important lessons within this book is to ensure you have control of your list. It is your most valuable asset. You should protect it from others, nurture it to grow and if inclined, sing to it every night because it's through this list you will generate the majority of your success.

There are several ways to obtain a visitor's contact information but the three most common ways are as follows.

## 1. Squeeze Pages

As the name suggests, the purpose of this page is to squeeze contact information from the visitor. It can also be referred to as a lead magnet. I know it could sound better but that's how it's known in the industry. The concept is for people to give you their contact details (opt in) so they can receive information from you. This is usually done by offering something of value first.

However, just remember that in today's society, it's easier to have your credit card replaced than your email address so people are much more averse to sharing if they don't first trust you. A good way to build trust is to first offer a gift without expectation. When you ask for someone's contact information, it is no longer a gift; it's a transaction, albeit a free one. By creating a genuine gift, you build rapport. If people want to know more, you can give them the option to enter their details rather than being forced.

Remember though, as I said at the start, you want to capture details before they leave the page. The truth is there is no right or wrong way to do this, just so long as you are doing it by providing something of value to justify opting in.

## 2. Free Membership

Another great way to get people's contact information is to offer them value that is locked behind a membership area. To gain access, they must first create a free account and thus give you their contact information. You can't market to these people via email legally unless they first say it's ok. Doing this is as simple as placing a small tick box on the registration page that says "Please keep me updated."

## 3. Online Support

Using chat boxes, ticketing systems or forums on your website is an effective way for people to reach out and contact your support department. (Even as a solopreneur I recommend creating a support department. It allows you to detach from other roles within the business.) You can take an email address in order to give a reply if you are not online and once you have answered their question, you can give them the option to opt in to your future correspondence.

A fourth option to obtain contact information is by purchasing it. The reason I am not including details here is due to the many concerns about purchasing legitimate databases and how to market to cold traffic. It would require an additional book just to cover enough detail that I would feel comfortable sharing.

A few years back, I was working with a company in central London. They hired me to consult and build their online presence. What really attracted me at the time was the very impressive list that they had purchased. Now I'll be honest back then, my ego was excited to tell people that we had a database of over 85 million people. That's some list! People came flocking to try and get their hands on it. For me, it was amazing to see just how desperate some people were and what lengths they would go to in the effort to create a shortcut in business, no matter how unethical. I say this not to scare you but to make you aware that some people will challenge you. How you position yourself now will determine how long you last in business.

So back to this list. The company set out a way to clean the list, ensure that it was optimised and that we were not spamming anyone or sending messages to people who didn't want to be contacted. Once done, the initial database had shrunk to approximately 20 million. Still more traffic than we knew what to do with. We were all going to be millionaires!

So we started sending out the emails. To accurately test our systems and the content within the messages, we only sent emails to 100,000 people initially in bursts of 10,000. Of those contacted, nothing happened. We assumed a glitch, tested all the systems and sent to a different 100,000. Still nothing. From sending out over 200,000 emails, we had generated exactly zero in revenue.

I learnt at this point that I would rather have a list of 1,000 raving fans who love and adore me, read every email, respond to every blog post and purchase every product than 100,000 people who have never heard of me.

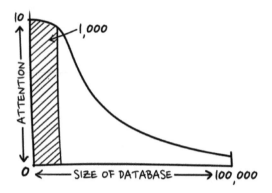

This is why I believe it is important to build your list rather than buy it. When you have to work hard to create and nurture, you have something people tend to respect more. You can pay attention to the customers more at the start and they become loyal brand ambassadors promoting your business, alerting you to challenges and forgiving you for mistakes.

From the moment you start to build your database, it's imperative that you understand this one very important concept:

**Your list is the lifeblood of your business.** It should be treated with the love and respect deserved by your first – born child. Never abuse your list by spamming or contacting them after a prolonged period of absence with a sales offer and never ever share the data from your list with anyone. It should never be sold or used for gain without all the subscribers' permission.

Once you have a system that is building your list, it is important to make sure you personally introduce yourself. The most common way to do this is to send regular emails using an auto responder (which we cover in more detail throughout Chapter 6). For the time being, it is a system that allows you to create a sequence of messages that are sent out at specific times after someone has subscribed to hear more from you.

I have a very simple rule when it comes to my list. I work hard to get people onto it initially and as soon as they sign up, I work as hard as I can to get them off. That may sound counter intuitive but what I mean by this is once they sign up to my main list I immediately start to segment them into categories relating to their specific wants and needs. The reason I do this is because generic emails rarely work– not as well as targeted emails. This is why list segmentation is one for the most important things you can do in your business and often it's overlooked.

Remember in Chapter 1 when I was talking about your target audience? The golf analogy? Let's consider how that same golf coach who is teaching professional golfers how to improve their game could segment his list.

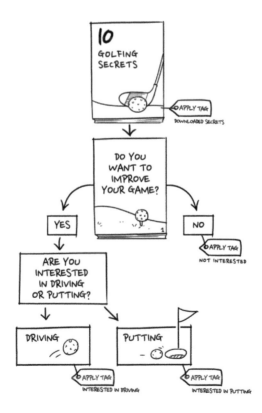

This golf coach has an opt−in gift on his website which teaches people the top ten secrets to improve their game overnight. This builds him a generic list of people interested in golf. He may send out an email asking if people are looking to improve their game and if they say yes, he could send another asking if they are weaker at driving or putting.

If you create a specific email about driving which is only sent to those interested in receiving it, do you think this would be more useful than a generic email to everybody? Can you also see how an email sent to people about putting when they are interested in driving might not be useful at all? By creating behaviour tags you can start to segment your list. A tag is like a sticky note attached to a visitor's profile. The more tags you have, the better you understand your visitor.

What you should aim to achieve here, as with our golf coach, is to find out as much information about the people who are in your database as possible, and segment them into smaller lists. The power of converting your subscribers into customers is based on your ability to segment your list and target specific interests with relevant valuable information.

## Initial Product Offer

Once you have your introduction sequence in place and you are segmenting your list, you might want to consider what is known as a "initial product offer." This is totally optional and would depend on your target audience and what you are selling. For products and services that are more expensive, it can be good to offer a lower−priced item first to build trust and rapport. This should be something simple or automated that allows people to invest in your business and see the value that you provide without worrying about the cost. After all, we could all take a risk spending £7 on something to find out if it's actually any good without much concern. However, at £497 people may have reservations purchasing it if they were unfamiliar with the person or business.

A perfect example of this is the book you are reading. This is my initial product offer. If I were to deliver this information one to one, it would cost substantially more, so my goal is to build a lasting relationship while I deliver a lot of value that makes a real difference in your business and your life. The question I asked myself when I started this journey was, "How can I add massive value to a large audience in a way that does not require my constant attention?" The answer was this book.

Your initial product should be one that is cost—effective. This is sometimes known as a loss—leader. It's a way of generating rapport and building trust. A potential customer should feel comfortable making a small investment with you to experience your sales process, your aftercare, the delivery in your product, the quality of your product and how you respond to support. It's this experience that will determine how likely your new customer is to continue purchasing from you and also how they will communicate with others about you. Whilst this section of the sales funnel will not generate massive profits for you, it is vital to ensure future success.

## Core Offer

What you will notice is that Online Mastery does exactly what I am telling you. If at any point you start to question if this works, then consider how my book is my initial product offer which gives you the opportunity to download the free workbook. This workbook also doubles as a lead magnet which allows me to connect with you and anyone you recommend it to. Once you have downloaded the workbook, you will receive a series of emails to ensure that you get the very best from this material. I will ask you questions over time that will paint a picture of who you are and what you need. My core offer is Build Your Website; a course that helps you implement the concepts you are reading about in the book. I do not hide this. I want you to see my process so that you can understand not only what I am doing but how I am doing it. By explaining this and you experiencing it, I hope you get ideas about how you can replicate this system within your business to achieve your own success.

There will be some people who come to you and will not be ready to purchase right away and there is nothing wrong when this happens. It helps to understand that people react differently depending on their thoughts, beliefs, environment and so many other factors. These may affect a purchase decision differently one day but not the next. Therefore, it makes sense to keep your brand in your audience's awareness. Just because they say "no" does not mean "no, never" it normally means "no, not now." Being clear about your intentions allows people to start a decision—making process that can last weeks or even months. If you take the opportunity to nurture these relationships until they are ready, you will find them the strongest allies in your marketing campaigns.

Customers who have experienced your sales funnel should now feel comfortable with you. Trust removes some of the common objections that people face when looking to purchase from someone they don't know. The outcome now is to identify their pain, show them that you understand it and offer a solution. The best way to provide authenticity and objection—handling is through case studies and testimonials. Using real live examples is a brilliant way to divert the pressure from the sales process and ensure that you remain confident and in control. Never appear desperate, needy, too accommodating, or anything that may hinder your chances of selling your core offer to a customer. There is great power in identifying customers who are not a good fit for your main services. It shows that you have pride and confidence in your ability and your service. People are drawn to that authenticity and in a world of noise, limiting who gets access to your core offer is often a good thing.

# Upsells

Do you remember at the start I said the purpose of your business is to make a profit? When someone comes to your website and decides to purchase a product or service, they will have their credit card out and be committed. Why would you not offer them something additional? There is no shame in upselling. When the golf coach sells lessons, he may well upsell a new set of golf balls, some new golf shoes or a membership to the golf club.

It's the most basic business principle that if someone is ready to buy something from you, offer them the next step in the journey. You can do it ethically. You don't need to force it upon them but just make them aware at the time of checkout that they can get access to the next step in your process. You should always have a next step! If nothing else, get them to show interest in a future service by putting their name on a waiting list. That way you're always growing.

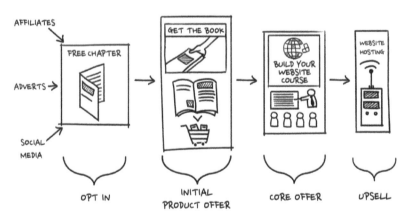

Can you see how the purchases progress in value? Now, some people will want to come straight in and take the full package with all the upsells. Others will need more time and want to progress through the journey. Some will never get past the start and you may find people jumping in at various points along the way. The goal here is to have a clear map of what you envisage to be your perfect customer journey and then test the results of what is working once you are live. You will find questions and activities to map this out in the workbook.

As we wrap up this chapter, keep in mind that the sales funnel is only one part of the customer journey, their interactions with you are a story and you get to write the script. Don't be scared about taking action. Just like everything else with your online presence, your customer journey can change and evolve–in fact, it should. I will leave you with the diagram which is a very basic overview of a customer journey and shows you a typical example of what you can expect as they move through your sales funnel.

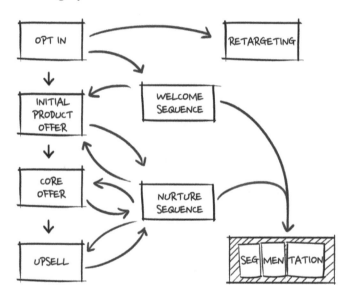

# CHAPTER 3
# SITEMAPS

If you type "site map" into Google, you will find that it's primarily used by search engines in order to list the structure and content of your website. It's also used by website visitors as an overview for quick access to areas of your site.

In reality, a sitemap is so much more than just these two things. For a long time, good developers have used them to build the layout and structure of a website. It effectively gives you a bird's eye view of what you are about to build and there is an abundance of amazing software that can assist you.

For me though, I like to do things differently.

I remember my first live event. People were coming through the door, introductions were being made and I could see the anticipation. Laptops were set up and everyone was waiting excitedly as I opened day one. A group of entrepreneurs had come together to learn how to build a website in a weekend. Keen and eager they sat, laptops open, ready to create their business–only to be startled when I told them to shut their laptops and put them away.

Most people are so used to working from technology they have forgotten the power of the pen.

The first thing I say to people who want to build a website is "Get offline!" You need to allow yourself to be creative and find your zone. I can't imagine Mozart composing some of his best symphonies with constant push notifications distracting him.

When we look at sitemaps, they can be overwhelming. After all, it's the big picture and it's not always something we can grasp right away. (Remember Will Smith and the wall.) The key here is just to make a start.

There are three types of sitemap. I just want to expand a little on each area. Then we will talk about where to focus your planning efforts.

## Type 1 – XML Sitemaps

This is a way to tell search engines who and where you are online. Crawlers, otherwise known as "spiders" or "robots" (which are just computer code), trawl the internet looking for links so that they can index all the websites. A quicker way to get noticed is to submit a document to the search engine telling them where everything is.

## Type 2 – HTML Sitemap

The HTML sitemap is used by your site visitors. It is a page within your site that users can visit to get quick access to all areas of your website. This is normally created in a text format with minimal design and categorised to allow the user easy navigation. You can hide certain aspects from this sitemap if you don't want them to find pages that are part of a process (like a thank you page which will only be available after they opt in to a sequence).

## Type 3 — Information Architecture

This type of sitemap is for developers to create an overview of all the pages that will make up the website. It's effectively what happens when you zoom out from the sales funnel to encompass the additional pages that you require.

In this chapter, we are going to focus on the third type of site map for architecting information. The outcome for creating this, as explained above, is to establish the big picture of your website. It gives you a clear sense of the scope of your project, how many pages you will require, what navigation will be used, how certain aspects of the website can be grouped together, and how the customer will glide effortlessly through the customer journey.

Let's dive into a typical sitemap.

One of the concepts in the diagrams from Chapter 2 was "traffic" and how people find you.

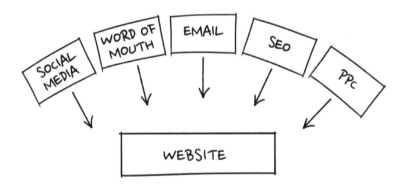

If you ever had the pleasure of visiting London's Oxford Street around December, you will know that the big shops like Harrods and Selfridges put on exquisite window displays. The creativity draws attention from all over the world. In a traditional shop, you have to enter through the front door before you can locate the cashier. Your website is slightly different in the sense that no one has to visit the homepage. A common misconception is that the homepage should contain everything about your website. In reality, a visitor might arrive through landing pages, blog posts, image searches, or videos, and never even see your homepage. It's important, therefore, to understand that your visitor can get very overwhelmed, very quickly if you do not plan a strategic system to achieve your outcome.

Landing pages are specifically designed to focus on one sales funnel. They target one specific audience and normally have one outcome. Whereas your homepage or "shop window" may be generic, your landing pages can get straight to the point. The great thing about starting your sitemap with the homepage is how it gives everything a sense of centre. We can establish the main pages which will attach to the homepage, typically the about us page, contact, blog, product or services and ideally a "get started" section. Once you have identified these top level pages you can understand the order they go and this becomes your navigation menu.

For this example, I am going to use my own website www.onlinemastery.co.uk to demonstrate how I would create a simple sitemap and so you can see the outcome.

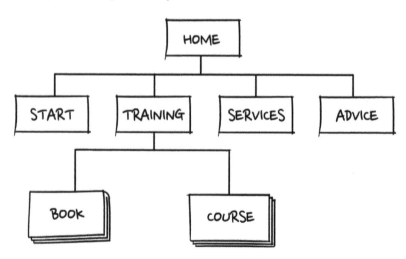

After the top level navigation, I have two landing pages: one for my book (Plan Your Website), and one for my course (Build Your Website). I've identified my sales funnels by changing the design on the sitemap to show a stack of pages (which I explain soon). You could visit the homepage and learn about the book or course there, but you ultimately are directed back to the appropriate landing page so you can find out more information. So at this stage, someone could visit my website from the homepage or via targeted advertising traffic they could be directed straight to my book sales funnel, bypassing all the distractions.

Once the visitor clicks to the landing page, we can take them deeper into the journey through the sales funnel and explain what options are available. Depending on which option they select, they will get closer to the end of the process.

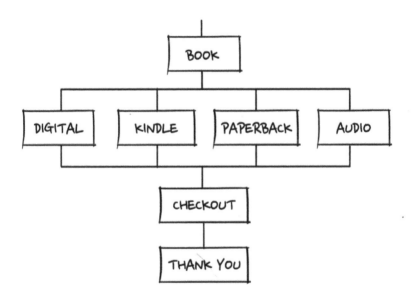

Always ask yourself, "What is next for my visitor?" When someone is on your website and clicks a specific button like "Learn More About My Book," then he moves further along the customer journey.

If he lands on the book page, what's next? If he chooses the digital book version, what's next? If he checks out with a credit card, what's next? And if he doesn't do any of those things and just stays on the homepage, what's next for him?

The idea is that you consider the question but still keep the sitemap basic, clutter free and to the point. It would be exhausting to map out every single page but you have to flesh out the minimum types of pages that are required. For example, if you have 10,000 products, you should not create 10,000 individual pages on your sitemap. Simply create one icon that represents a large number of pages, similar to this:

Once you have your sitemap, you will have a much better idea of the size of your project. Not only will this help the developer consider how to stay within your budget, but it will also eliminate "scope creep." (This is a term developers use when a client keeps saying, "Can you just...?" this almost always adds additional time and cost to a project and often disheartens the developer.)

I want to share a story about how creating a sitemap saved one of my clients from wasting both time and money. He had been offered a website through a business in the commercial catering industry. When we sat down to plan the scope of this project, the first thing we looked at was how many products were going to be sold. It was in excess of 20,000 (considerably more than the average ecommerce website) and there were several challenges that came with the project. Aside from performance concerns was that of the customer's usability experience, specifically the navigation, and how I would create a system that could easily search for these products and showcase them in friendly way.

As it happened with this client, when we built the site there was a main menu (the top level navigation) and a series of submenus, and sidebar menus. It quickly became quite complex. Without the sitemap to refer back to, it would have become very overwhelming. Also at a later date after the system was built, it was useful to have a reference point so we could test the functionality. We could easily look back and see what we created. This gave us an easy way to cross reference with our sitemap to make sure we had not missed anything.

A sitemap not only gives the clarity of the overall journey but it gives you the confidence that what you are creating is right, rather than actually creating it and asking, "Is it right?"

Sketch it out on paper first. Lay out the sitemap and know it is right—before you even spend any money or time actually building it. It's better to change things in the design stage than to get it wrong in the development phase. Having a sitemap will help you uncover and identify any challenges, weaknesses or other considerations on a grander scale.

You'll find a series of activities to lead you through this in the workbook.

# CHAPTER 4
# WIREFRAMES

The purpose behind having a wireframe is to visually see the layout of your specific pages before you create them. In the last chapter we created an overview, so now we are going to focus on the individual pages, the elements within them, and how they relate to each other, specifically on different devices. Below is the sitemap that was created from the previous chapter.

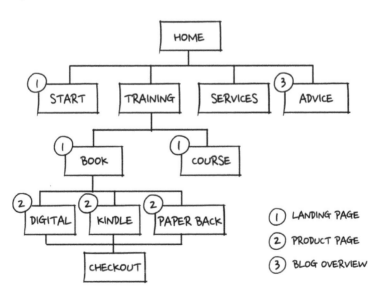

Every type of page needs its own page template, but it is efficient to look over the sitemap and identify groups of pages that have the same layout. For example, if you have an ecommerce business, the shop would have one layout and the products another. However, all the products would normally share the same product template, but the blog roll would need a third style.

As you can see from the next diagram, I have added a legend to my site map which identifies some of the wireframes required. (1, 2 and 3) The book uses a landing page template but once the customer clicks to purchase, they are taken to a screen with options for the digital, Kindle or paperback versions. These all use the same page template so it only needs to be created once. I personally like to use a numbered legend. Some people use different shapes and some use colours. There is no right or wrong way to do this, it's personal preference.

At its core, a website is made up of invisible containers, but for simplicity I'll call them boxes. We use them to contain images, videos, headlines, text and other elements. We can combine multiple boxes both next to and within each other to customise the look and feel of the webpage. They are referred to by developers as divisions or the correct HTML code is <div>. They can be given their own label so you can identify and edit them later. The code would look like this

<div id="example">content goes here</div>

Don't worry! I'm not going to teach you how to code but I do think it's very helpful for you to know a bit about how it works. By targeting the "ID" of the div, we can customise it using cascading style sheets (CSS) which is why I urge you to get a very basic understanding of HTML and CSS so that you can make simple changes if you need to. A great website to help you with this is www.w3schools.com and you would only need one day to start understanding the fundamentals.

# Best Practice

There is no right or wrong way to create a wireframe but there are some things you should consider. When you are building one, it is best not to use colour, images, custom fonts or anything that is going to visually represent your actual website. The purpose here is to create boxes that show you the layout of your content and the customer journey within the page. They are also to show your developer the placement of elements and how they will interact with each other. The more simplistic the line art you use here, the better, as it gives you a chance to focus on usability and what happens when the page size is changed.

As we briefly touched on before, websites use a programming language called HTML. It is this code that the search engines use when looking at your site (it's a bit like The Matrix). One thing that helps you to optimize your website for the search engines is the ability to structure your content correctly.

We can give specific <div> tags a title if they are related to the structure of the webpage. This helps not only identify the layout better but also helps search engines organize your content better.

It starts with the Header <header>, is followed by the navigation <nav>, then the main content area <section> which would be broken down into separate <articles> of content. Next to the articles is the option for a sidebar <aside> and finally the footer <footer>.

Now you can add, remove or change any of these elements but overall, and for the purpose of simplicity, we are going to use a standard example:

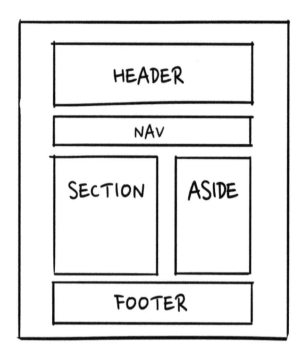

It can become problematic when people don't use wireframes to organise their content. With no clear or defined outcome for a page, visitors are just left to fend for themselves and often disengage with a site before they have a chance to see its true value.

When you are considering the content within a page, it helps to understand the best way of structuring it. This is something often overlooked due to haste, carelessness or a general lack of understanding. While you are mapping out the overall structure and elements that will be used, it's important to also consider the headlines.

Standard code on a website supports six headline variations, <h1> through to <h6>. Typically, <h1> is used for your main page title, <h2> is for all your subtitles and <h3> if there is further need to breakdown the article. This not only improves your search engine optimisation (SEO) but also makes the content flow better and gives you the opportunity to consider what is important for the page.

Below is a basic wireframe of a homepage:

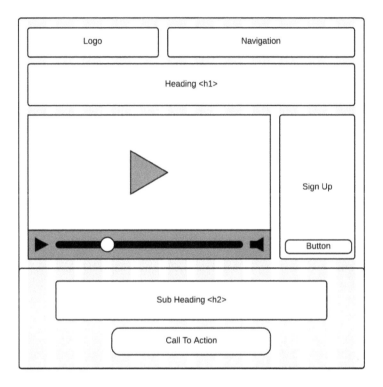

It's very easy to move things about in the early stages and there are fantastic tools online which create wireframes. The challenge I see so often is when someone builds a website first and then tries to move things. It can be quite difficult, especially in the latter stages. Imagine that your designer has already created something for you and now you ask for changes — this adds time and unexpected cost to your project.

## Responsive Design

When smartphones developed the ability to view websites, they changed the game of web design. For a long time, people would not consider designing a website for mobile phones and even today some websites still are not mobile friendly. If a website is "unresponsive," then the elements on the webpage do not respond to different screen sizes. When I started building websites, everything was designed to be a fixed width. Developers knew exactly how many pixels were on the screen. Logos, headings and all the content used to be fixed in one place. It was simple.

Nowadays, it's not possible to tell who is going to view your website or what device they will use. With phones, tablets, laptops, desktops and everything in between, you must have the end user in mind when creating your page. People would rather have simple designs that work than complex ones that look bad on smaller devices. Something you should really consider at this stage is that one page might require multiple wireframes each for different—sized devices.

A popular framework that utilises responsive design is a series of columns that are known as "a grid." Most responsive web designers use a twelve—column grid layout. This was made famous by a framework called "bootstrap" because it gives great flexibility when developing. In this example, a mobile will use four columns, a tablet six, and a desktop twelve. With this layout, you can start to structure your responsive wireframes for different devices.

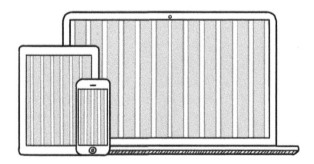

This grid layout also gives the ability to visualise how elements will react with each other when the screen is made smaller. I used a basic wireframe throughout this chapter so I could represent a series of elements and how they appear on a mobile, tablet and desktop screen. A responsive website stacks the <div> containers on top of each other when the browser is resized; non responsive sites do not change. Instead the page is cut off or becomes too small when resized.

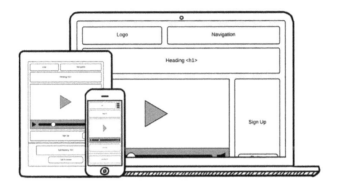

There are typically two types of responsive layouts for a grid. Both have pro's and con's and your choice depends on your preference. "Fixed layouts" are generally easier to use and customise in terms of design but can create excessive white space on a page. "Fluid layouts" are typically more user− friendly because they adapt to the device they are being viewed on, but the designer will have less control over what the user sees. This creates a divide between designer (who wants the site to look good) and developer (who wants the site to function correctly). I would personally always choose customer usability over everything else. But, to get a great website and be successful, you need to account for both.

The screen on a device is known as a "viewport" and rather than try to cater for every screen, the industry standard is to select four main sizes known as breakpoints. These are pixels which are set to a fixed width. They affect the display by forcing the layout to change as the screen gets narrower.

To be classified as responsive, a website needs at least two breakpoints: one for very narrow screens like mobiles and another for medium — width screens like tablets. Ideally, you should set at least four breakpoints and this will evolve as technology improves. At the time of writing this book, there are four main sizes you should consider: mobile, tablet, desktop, and widescreen.

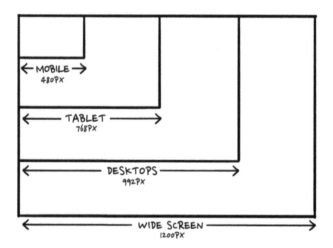

This illustration shows the different viewports and the current industry standard breakpoints.

Check the workbook for the most up — to — date viewports. On occasion, there may be a specific device that needs attention and you can set additional breakpoints. But this is on a case by case basis and it's not something to worry about. You can't possibly cater for every device. There are already too many and this will only increase.

Another interesting change in the way good developers work is they now build a website for the mobile first. This means that instead of building a website and then stripping it back for the mobile phone, they start with the mobile phone and build the site with only what is needed. From there, they add features as the screen size increases.

I personally believe it's far better to add value rather than take it away. It also ensures that your content is relevant depending on the device. For example, a restaurant website may want to show you a booking form, opening times and high resolution images of the food from the website. However, key features for the mobile version might be a map and contact number—because these are things that customers would want if they were trying to locate the restaurant. Understanding what would serve your customers best is at the heart of good design and it's much easier to do now at this stage than to try and pull things apart later.

In the workbook, we dive into how to create a wireframe and give you some great examples that you can use for building your own site. It takes me on average fifteen minutes to mock up a wireframe these days so don't be overwhelmed with the process. Remember I will take you through everything step by step.

# CHAPTER 5
# CONTENT

Who are you talking to and what are you saying to them? These are the two main questions you should be asking yourself when considering your content.

*"Content is king." ~ Bill Gates*

I believe Bill was right for a long time but now a new approach is required. I say this because in just one minute:

- 300 hours of video are uploaded to YouTube
- 347,222 tweets are sent on Twitter
- 31 million messages are sent on Facebook
- 204 million emails are sent
  *(Statistics from Data Never Sleeps 3.0, Domo.com)*

With this abundance of information we need to find a way of standing out. I truly believe the new saying "Context is King" is more relevant to becoming successful online. Context is all about understanding the unique interests and needs of each visitor at any given time. The best way to get noticed in a vast and busy world is to create great content with outstanding value that resonates with your target audience.

Many people have tried and failed to find methods of avoiding content creation but search engines have become very good at identifying what is genuine. Remember, a website is only ever going to be seen by one person at a time. You should aim to create your content as "one to one" and not "one to many." This mind – set will allow you to make your message personal to the reader and not like they are just a number in a system. Pay extra care and attention here because this is going to make or break your success online.

This is a good thing. It causes you to think about what you produce rather than mindlessly adding to the abundance of information. If you can create a compelling voice in the sea of noise, then you will be heard. It just needs to be one that is congruent with who you are and one that resonates with your target audience. The best way to achieve this is through stories. Since birth we have been surrounded by stories. It's what connects us to each other. Your story can either be one of inspiration or desperation and how you portray it will depend upon the visitor that you attract.

There are two audiences, both equally important, for whom you must write your content. The first is the human audience, the person who is going to read the content, relate to the content, and be impacted by it.

For this reason, you need to create a message that connects to your target audience. Your content will not resonate with everyone, nor should it. You should strive to tell people what they NEED to hear, not what they WANT to hear. It should drive them to take action, sign up, purchase or do anything else that directs them towards identifying and solving their problem.

The second audience we are going to create our content for are search engines. It would be a huge mistake not to optimise content that will establish your presence organically otherwise known as SEO.

# Content for People

So let's first look at the human element of content and the creation process specifically because you should not delegate it, especially not at first. The reason I suggest being involved in this yourself is because nobody will know your audience as well as you. If you are going to create a business in a niche with a specific target audience, then you should be positioning yourself as an expert within that industry. As a result, nobody will be able to create the content in the same way that you, regardless if you are good at writing or not. Whilst you may get somebody else to proofread or to produce it later on, in the initial stages, you should be very much involved in the process. People prefer to buy from *people*, even if they are dealing with a company. It is usually through an interaction with a person that this connection is formed.

In my opinion, there is no better way to start this than to get a pen and paper or open up a text document and just start writing. Even if you are not very good, it does not matter at this stage. What you write down now may not be what gets used at a later date, but you need to start getting your content out. You may decide to have a content writer or team to manage this. Maybe, like me, you dislike writing but that doesn't mean you can't find another way.

When I wrote this book, I had real trouble getting the words out. My way of overcoming this challenge was to list some bullet points and think about speaking to my customer avatar. Then I got a microphone, connected it to the computer and started to talk about the things I wanted in the book. The result of this was an audio file which could be sent to a company who would transcribe it. Once back I would edit the document until it was how I wanted. Finally, I sent it to an editor to double check for mitsakes before being overlooked by a proof — reader and finally published. I know there is still room for improvement but it was all about getting to 80%. Be resourceful to get the outcome you want and so even if writing isn't your thing, look at another way to get your outcome.

*"Perfection itself is imperfection."* ~ *Vladimir Horowitz*

With content you should aim to cover four stages in the visitor's journey. Market to get attention, engage so they stay and read, relate so they want more and follow up to keep them interested.

Ask yourself what content needs to be created. There are many different types, and in the workbook, you'll see recommendations for working through these in order. A few examples that you need to start with are:

- a clear and compelling headline
- a slogan for your business
- your mission statement or biography
- headlines and descriptions for additional pages
- content or articles for the pages you create
- blog post content
- legal pages like "privacy policy" and "terms & conditions"
- marketing content to promote your website
- email content to nurture your list
- social media updates
- press releases

If you read this book first, you will see I cover headlines in this chapter but the workbook explains things in much greater detail.

When creating content, I always consider if it is viable to record a video first. A video can be repurposed in many ways whereas text cannot. You not only have the **video** but you can take screenshots for **images**, extract the **audio** and have it transcribed into **text**. You will find what works for you and what your target audience prefer as you test variations.

## Headlines

We know who our target audience are from the strategies in Chapter 1, so now your focus should be on the first written message your visitors see. This can be in an advert, on your website or through a nurture process but It should be something that says "Hey! You're in the right place to solve your problem!" (I recommend that you choose better words to do this!)

With any content that you create the goal should be to do two things: hook them and guide them.

Let's look at what happens when someone lands on your website as an example. At the top of the page, there should be a headline. It's good to pique curiosity at this point so they continue to read. Be thought – provoking by focusing more on a message that reaches the creative, emotional, right side of the brain. Less is often more here. Don't make it too clever or complicated. Some of the biggest brands in the worlds all use three or four words for their headline. Just remember success sounds simple!

Once you have your headline, you should consider a sub – headline. This is for the more left – brain and it's rational need to understand, so give a more logical explanation here. You will do well to focus on the outcome and help the reader to know they are in the right place.

The heading is known as "the hook." it can be about anything as long as it is interesting, unique and makes the reader curious so they carry on reading.

Here are some great examples of big brands using simple headlines and subheadings to hook their target audience:

**Uber**
Your Ride, On Demand.
Transportation in Minutes with the uber app

**Spotify**
It's Play Time
Get the Right Music, Right Now

**Netflix**
Time to Unwind
Kick off your shoes and put on a film

Another great website that uses this tactic well is airbnb.

Their headline is Welcome Home and it provokes curiosity and can make the reader think about home (which in most cases has the added feel—good factor). When we look at the sub—headline, it reads "Rent unique places to stay from local hosts in 190+ countries." As you can see, the title doesn't give much away, the subtitle gives a little more clarity so people who are travelling and need a place to sleep know they can find a solution.

Once visitors know this website is right for them, they are "hooked," and the next way we can help them is by guiding them. This can be achieved with a call to action or "CTA" which is something very clear (normally a clickable button) that tells the visitor what to do next. In terms of this airbnb example, it's the high—contrast search icon which draws your eye.

Because they know their target audience, they can create a very specific message. As a result, this page only has one outcome and is free from clutter, making it a more pleasurable experience for the user.

We live in an age where everyone is fighting for our attention. Did you know that on average you are subjected to over 20,000 different brands a day? Just look around and see how many different labels you can see right now, and that's before they start trying to compete for your attention. The world is saturated with advertising and marketing to the point where people are becoming numb to traditional methods. Businesses are becoming more creative to gain the attention of potential customers and through all of this, you can be certain that less is more.

Gone are the days of really text—heavy websites. Of course, text helps with your optimisation for the search engines, but people's attention spans are a lot shorter than they used to be. As a result, people like to read small blocks of easy to digest text. Just go on to Apple's website for a great example. When you look at their new product releases, the first thing they show are crisp images with just a small paragraph of text pointing out the key benefits.

When people come to your website, they are not going to want to read (not until they know it is worth their time to be on your website). When they first land, they are going to want to have a quick flick through to make sure it's for them. If something gets their attention, they may then explore further. Have something very simple at the outset, so when they land on the page, they can identify with it. As they go deeper, like on the product pages and in product descriptions or blog, then you can start to include more content.

You also need to ensure that when writing your content, you avoid too much terminology. If I were to sit here and talk to you with all the jargon that web designers use about PHP,

JavaScript and using EM instead of PX, you may glaze over, not understand or find it overwhelming. It is a really good idea to imagine your customers and how they will perceive the content that you are creating for them.

One critical yet overlooked area of content are the legal documents that you need to include on your site, namely your Terms and Conditions and Privacy Policy. These often are linked to in your footer, or when people make important decisions, like during the checkout process.

## Content for SEO

The next area we are going to look at regarding content is search engine optimisation. When a search engine lands on your website, it uses technology called a "web crawler" (also known as a "bot" or a "robot").

The search engines send these bots onto the world wide web so they can track links and gather all the information on the relevant pages, and then index it back to their database. You can accelerate this process by creating an XML sitemap on your website and submitting it directly to the search engine, effectively telling them where all your links are.

When the bots land on your site, they will check for a number of things. Firstly, that the website is built properly using the correct structure, and your site does not contain any errors. During this time, they will also look for known viruses or malicious code that could result in your website being placed on a blocked database. (You may have seen warning pages before if you have tried to visit potentially harmful websites.) If the code is good, they will check the performance of the site. As a society, we expect everything instantly and search engines work hard to provide this for its customers. If your site is slow, there is a higher chance it will be placed lower in the search results. Finally, the bots will look at the content, specifically the "meta data" which is a summary of the content within that page.

If you have a poorly designed website, don't understand SEO or are too lazy to optimise your content, then you are going to be missing out on some very important organic traffic that could come to your website from the search engines for free. On an average page, you should be looking to write a minimum of 400 words.

## Using Keywords in Content

Keywords are either single words or phrases that describe additional content. They can apply to an overall page on your website or specific media like images, videos and text. Keywords are a great reason why it is so important to have a customer avatar at this point. If you can understand the mindset of your visitors, then you can start to relate with how they may be feeling, how they might be acting and more precisely what they might be looking for when they type into a search engine.

Someone who is in pain or stressed might be asking different questions on search engines compared to someone who is calm and relaxed. It helps to understand the mindset of your audience so that you can predict what they might be typing. That way you can get your website in front of them. If, for example, I suffer with headaches, I may visit a search engine and type in "how to stop headaches" or "fast pain relief for headaches." Or if I'm more of a holistic person who doesn't believe in traditional pharmaceutical intervention, I may search for "holistic remedies for headaches" or "alternative ways to stop headaches."

If your website content is optimized for these keywords and your website is bot friendly, your site will make it into the search results. How high you rank on the page depends on how much competition is fighting for the same keywords.

It's possible to choose keywords that you think are good but underperform. These are known as "perceived keywords." For example, the word "dieting" could be part of totally different search strings: "tired of dieting," "secrets for effective dieting," "no more dieting," etc. You need to be as specific as you can be when you are identifying which keywords to use; individual words will give you a broad or general result whereas phrases will give you a more targeted result. This is because when you string keywords together to create parts of a sentence, you create a more unique keyword and it's easier to be seen by the specific people who are looking for what you offer.

You can actually find out, before you start creating something, if there is even a demand for it. You should know whether people are actually searching for the services you will offer. How receptive will your audience be and how much traffic can you expect to get? How much competition is there for these keywords? Keyword research is really valuable pre — work. There is no point in creating something if there is no demand.

## Other Content to Consider

Once you have your site content, there are two other areas that you will need to consider creating content for: marketing and nurturing.

For marketing the only real factor to consider is consistency. Of course other elements will play a role in the success of your advertising campaigns but consistency is key. If you blog once a week, then make sure you always blog on the same day at the same time. Readers will start to anticipate your content and know when it's coming. As humans, we are creatures of habit and we like things that are familiar. Regarding social media, you will need to test your target audience. Start by sending updates at different times and monitoring the response. Find a time that works best and use that for your updates.

For me, marketing is sometimes a challenge because of a very busy schedule so I have to plan and prepare everything I do. This is my secret formula for creating successful content and I share it as an idea if you want to have more freedom in your diary and still ensure you are presenting yourself to your audience.

Every time I get a new idea for marketing I add it to a list. On the last day of the month, I take either the top topic on the list or one that is trending in relation to my industry or news and I plan out four separate videos. I record them on the fly, each one between three to five minutes in length.

I then give the videos to my team who transcribe the content for me into a text document. I also give a link to the videos, some reference material, and any added notes to my editor and they create a well—phrased, 400—word blog post (that is keyword specific) for that chosen topic. I review the post to ensure it sounds like me and that it has my spin. The post is then dissected into social media updates with text and images that are relevant and loaded into an editorial calendar. Sometimes I repurpose the audio from the video to create a podcast. The process takes a full day but it gives me a month's worth of fully automated content and I can focus on other areas of the business.

Once people have subscribed to your list, you are going to need content to introduce yourself and set the expectations of what they can expect you to deliver. You will also need content to engage and nurture them. Once they purchase a product or service from you it might be a good idea to create a series of aftercare content that really adds value to the whole experience.

A quick tip if you are struggling to create your content is to talk with a real person who is similar to one of your customer avatars. Ask them if you can record your talk. Once you are in flow, it is much easier to create. You just need to identify the best to inspire you.

## Conclusion

Content is communication and it requires context.

You may feel at this point that there is a lot to create. You're right. But as I explained at the start with Will Smith and the wall, it's all about one brick at a time, one article at a time and one page at a time.

This is something that will continuously evolve. The great thing about online communication is that you can create a journey that others can follow. They can grow with you and the best way to attract raving fans into your business is to create genuine heartfelt content that resonates with the reader.

# CHAPTER 6
# DESIGN

This section is often overlooked. Website developers usually do not know what design entails, nor should they. A common misconception is that a developer will be able to design a website as well as code it. People who are skilled in development are logical problem solvers and primarily use the left side of their brain. The same person is not likely to be as creative as someone who uses the right side of their brain. So when you start looking for a website developer, consider that you may also need a website designer.

Even within design, there are graphic designers, illustrators, and branding experts, just to name a few. (There are also very important distinctions between a graphic designer who works on printed publications and someone who designs websites.) Digital images are created differently to print. Not all designers have experience with responsive design or making images "web ready," and that alone could make a huge difference on your website. Also, many designers can take a concept you give them and create something— but what they might not be able to do is advise you what is right for your business. An illustrator, for example, may not understand branding and as a result, may not know how to create designs that resonate best with your target audience. Let me just be clear: I am not saying that you need to hire an entire team to manage different elements of your design and build. I'm just giving you some things to consider before moving forward.

# The Purpose of Design

Before we dive into website design, we should really consider what design is. It is not just about pretty pictures on a page but the actual feelings visitors get when they encounter your brand. This process can start long before they visit your website and in order to plan for success, you need to consciously create their first impression and how they will perceive you. Once they land on your website, the biggest aspect of design, aside from how it looks, is the user experience or "UX." This is why wire framing is so important to provide an initial understanding of how elements on a page will interact with each other.

# Branding

A brand is simply a way to distinguish one business from another. I've had conversations with people who think having a brand is just for big companies, or that branding is a scary process. Actually, creating your brand identity can be a lot of fun because the brand is where your personality and unique qualities can be expressed. In the workbook, I mention some places to get more help with this, but for now, let's just focus on the essentials which will help you create your brand guidelines.

## Colour Psychology

This is the study of how colour influences human perception and emotion. It has been used by marketing agencies for many years. They understand that by using colour we can evoke a reaction from the viewer. This is because colours can have different meanings— trust, integrity, wealth, spirituality, honesty, femininity or masculinity. Whatever your core values, there is a colour that psychologically represents what it is you're trying to convey so it's important to understand your target audience so you can relate to them. Far too often I see people choosing colours they like and not because it's best for the business.

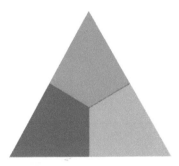

For digital design, we start with three colours: red, green and blue. By mixing these colours, we can increase the palette to have additional colours. When we expand this further, we get a wheel of colours from which to choose our online identity.

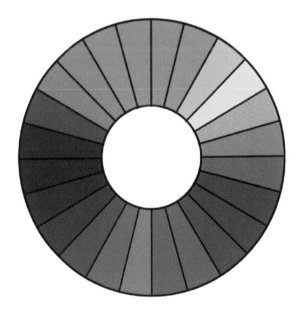

For your website design itself, you should focus on just three colours. You need a primary, secondary and a call to action colour. The first two should be next to each other on the colour wheel whilst the call to action should be opposite so that it draws attention and stands out.

I'll give you a quick example for our golf coach. On his website, he is using blue as his primary colour, green as his secondary colour and red as his call to action. Below you can see the colour palette that he uses throughout his brand for his website and marketing material. The core values that this exhibits are trust, strength and security from the blue, growth and balance from the green (which is also the easiest colour for the eyes to process) and excitement, energy and power from the red call to action.

It's also important to consider the tone of the colour at this stage. Are you looking for loud vibrant colours or soft pastel colours? Each can create a feeling in the viewer so understanding your target audience and how they feel will impact which colours represent your business. After all, they will be the people spending the most time on your website.

## Typography

Font selection is a very important aspect of the design phase because it conveys another element of your website's character. The message that you deliver in your content is literally delivered via your fonts. Ensuring you get the right typography for your site and marketing material is very important for your first impression. Also, remember that too many fonts can be distracting. You should limit yourself to a maximum of two or three fonts.

Have you ever visited a website and just thought "Wow!"? Chances are, you initially reacted to the colour palette, typography and images being used to extend the message. It is by no chance luck or an accident. Whilst you may not have the budget for a professional design team, having a basic awareness of these concepts will give you the edge over someone who is just throwing up a website without real care or passion.

## Consistency

One of the most important things to consider about the design of your online presence is making sure you are creating familiarity. This can be achieved by using the same profile picture and the same cover image across social media channels (not to be confused with using the same content). Different social media channels require different content but the design of your online presence can remain consistent. Use the same colour palette and fonts throughout your website and even in your email templates, so that when you communicate (social media posts, blog articles, your email newsletters or something via direct mail), they relate to you. They know it's you because the colours, the logo, the images and everything matches.

## Your Logo

A logo is an important way to build familiarity with your brand. Although not required, it can convey a powerful message and become the face of your business. It is therefore recommended to take some time when creating a logo to ensure it is relevant to your target audience.

There are three main types of logo to consider:

**Iconic** – These use imagery to relate to your business. Often these are the most recognisable brands in the world because a symbol can stand on it's own, even without the brand name. Examples of this are the Nike swoosh, Apple's logo or the Twitter bird.

**Wordmark** – These communicate the essence of your brand through typography. The subtle personality differences of fonts should never be underestimated. Examples of this are Google, Disney and Coca Cola.

**Combination Mark** – These combine the Iconic and Wordmark logos. This is the most common type of logo because it blends the power and recognition of an image with the company name. Examples of this are Intel, NASA and Ford.

If you're going to commission a logo, you should consider a few things. It needs to look good on your website but it may also need to be printed out or applied to clothing and merchandise. Something that works on screen with lots of shading cannot be easily embroidered on a t—shirt. Enlarging your logo for the purpose of displaying it on a banner, billboard or the side of a building is something else to consider. For that, you need to request a scalable, or "vector," logo. A vector image is based on mathematical proportions. As such, you can make it as big as you want. It's very important that your logo is simple enough that it can be vectorised.

# Website Ready Images

It is common for people to use stock media sites for images. Even images that have been created by a professional designer can sometimes be much larger than what is required for your website. I've seen countless times when someone uploads an image with no editing for the web. The result is a large file size that loads slowly and uses up additional bandwidth. Don't forget who your target audience is or where they are. People using data plans whilst browsing on mobile phones sometimes have the challenge of slower connections and limited data packages.

We can optimize images for the web in several ways, this is called, "web ready." It would normally result in the image being reduced to a resolution of 150 PPI (Pixels Per Inch), compressed to 60% of its quality, and saved at the correct height and width. If you're going to use an image that's 300 by 300 pixels it would be a waste to upload it at 2000 by 2000 pixels. You can compress it down by making sure that the image resolution, quality and dimensions are correct.

Many designers will likely give you a web ready version of your graphics in one of the common file formats: JPEG or PNG. A jpeg image is a standard image and if it's going to live on a website, then request your designer create an image at a resolution of 150 PPI, as well as a specific width and height.

Images at 150 PPI are typically "retina ready," which is the new wave of very crisp, HD quality images. Some older browsers or older machines may not support retina, so you might consider scaling down to what is called 72 PPI. If you wanted something for print, then 300 DPI (Dots Per Inch) is the industry standard. Print uses a different measurement of pixels which is a much deeper conversation that I decided not to cover in this book.

Double check that your designer creates in Photoshop or Adobe Illustrator and ask for the raw files when the project is done— even if you don't have this software or lack the ability to open the source files. This way, if you want to make changes later, the same (or another) designer can pick up where the last one left off.

# Responsive Design

For many designers, responsive websites are a hassle. Designers want everything to be pixel perfect. They want every design element to have a permanent home. This is where functionality and design sometimes clash. It's really important to understand that a designer will look at things from a design perspective whereas a developer will look at something from a functionality standpoint. You need to incorporate both. There's no point creating something so clever or so beautiful that it won't display or function on different devices.

## Copyright Images

All too often, people use search engines to find images. It is safest to assume any images in search results are already copyrighted and not available for you to use on your website without prior consent from the artist. Just because you provide a reference does not mean that you are allowed to use that image and by hitting publish, you could be subjecting yourself to a considerable amount of trouble.

There are many services where you can purchase media that is "royalty free." This means that you are only required to pay for it once and not depending on how many times it is viewed. Some require ongoing licences. If the owner finds you using it without the appropriate licence they have to, by law, take action to have it removed. If you do hire someone to create images for you, then make sure you own the copyright and have written permission to use them.

## Budget

It is really important to set aside an amount in your budget for design. There are several different ways that you can approach the design phase. The main question to ask here is "Am I going to hire a branding consultant for my strategy and brand guidelines or am I going to create them myself?"

Once you have your guidelines, you need to decide "Am I going to hire a designer to create the project or will I do it myself?"

I strongly urge you at this point not to use some friend just because he or she has mocked up a couple of designs before. So many people fall into a trap of looking on Facebook for friends who can design. Your friend wants to help you, but in essence, unless your design is done professionally and properly, you're never going to get the level of service that you could by going to a person who treats you as a client (which is the way that you deserve to be treated, but is different from being a friend).

Another major decision is whether to use stock images and pre−made templates, or create a bespoke design. If something is bespoke, it's going to cost a lot more money than a template. It's not always necessary to invest in that level of customisation.

You do **not** need a fully−bespoke design to get started. These days, you can buy a theme that is pre−built and has all the design built into it. However, at the very minimum, I urge you to have the following key elements of your website designed specifically for you: the main banner for your website, your social media banner, your profile picture, your logo and any product images.

## What to Expect from a Designer

Unless you approach design with a strategy, then you're going to get what you ask for (which is not necessarily what you need or want). I've gone down the route before of using a well known freelancing website and looking specifically for the person with the most 5−star reviews and best credentials.

I actually hired a team and paid them a lot of money for the first Online Mastery logo that never got used. The reason was that I didn't have specific brand guidelines or a strategy in place. I told them what I thought I wanted and they designed it for me. We had a lot of back and forth: "I don't like this... I don't like that... I do like this." Eventually I settled on something. Within six months, I had it recreated.

If you reach out to a good designer they will first ask you questions relating to who you are, who your audience are and what message you are trying to create. We covered this in

Chapter 1. What they don't always expect is for a client to have the foresight to create wireframes, content and brand guidelines prior to initial contact. By doing this, you instantly establish yourself as someone who knows what they are doing. This reassures a good designer that working with you will be an enjoyable process.

To maximise your investment and allow a different level of creativity to unfold, these are the things you should have clarity on before you approach a potential graphic designer:

- Who your target audience is
- Colour palette
- Typography
- Sitemaps
- Wireframes
- Content

If a designer is not for you, then at least take on board this advice to make better decisions when creating your website. Everything mentioned in this chapter is to help you avoid banging a square peg into a round hole. Too often I see people who are convinced they need a website purchase a template and then try to ram content and random design elements together. A good graphic designer will not only ensure your website looks amazing, but that it does so on all devices.

## Conclusion

I spent so long searching for good designers who could understand my business and create concepts based on the thoughts inside my head. These designers are rare and I found that what I was looking for stretched well beyond website design and into the marketing phase of my business. Many people settle here for a template design or something they can fit their business into. There is nothing wrong with this approach but you will be more effective if you infuse your brand into the template and your marketing.

# CHAPTER 7
# SYSTEMS

Let's dive into the nuts and bolts of your website and what will actually be used to create it. So far, we have talked a lot about strategy and planning. It's time to decide what functionality and features we will add to automate and better serve both yourself and your visitors.

In this chapter, we're going to talk about the systems which are used to make your website function. Some of these include your website's operating system, any e–commerce solutions or complementary programs, auto responders and much more. This could become very overwhelming, so in an attempt to keep it simple, I'll just give an overview of the different systems, functionality and things to consider. However, I'll break down more specific topics in the workbook so that you can go deeper if you desire.

A website is online 24 hours a day, 7 days a week, 365 days a year. It therefore makes sense to maximize its potential to grow your business. Any point in the customer journey where you are involved reduces your ability to grow. In most cases, potential customers want instant answers, so it makes sense to create systems that assist them in getting what they want. When someone can book an appointment or buy something online without needing human interaction, then you have the ability to scale. Of course, I recommend a human touch in the process, but at least consider what can be automated and what requires your attention. The majority of leads can be pre—qualified without taking up your time.

With most systems, you have three options: build it yourself, buy it outright from somebody or rent it. You may remember I mentioned in Chapter 1 that the industry is shifting towards SAAS ("software as a service") which means that developers build and maintain the software and the system for a monthly or annual fee. Thankfully with SAAS, you don't have to worry about the maintenance, the cost of running the hardware, or fixing any bugs or problems. You just get to use the software. However, there may be some limitations in terms of what the system can do, and there is the ongoing cost to consider. You need to be absolutely certain that you can export your data and continue to run your business. It's really important when you're looking at a third party, you ask the questions, "What happens if I leave your service? Can I take my data with me?"

## Content Management Systems (CMS)

A CMS allows you to access a dashboard on your website—from this central interface, you can create, edit, organise or remove content, as well as maintain your website. I've spent tens of thousands of pounds on software for my websites and I've learnt a thing or two along the way. I taught myself how to code HTML and CSS from watching videos, reading books and pulling websites apart to see how they worked. I would spend hours, days and sometimes weeks learning tricks and tactics to make me a better developer.

When I was introduced to different CMS platforms, I was told using one was the equivalent of 10,000 hours of writing code. The question was, which one should I use? If you speak to a developer and ask them what to use, someone who specializes in custom—built systems will tell you that you need a custom built system. Somebody who works with WordPress will recommend using WordPress. Joomla developers will say Joomla is the best, and Drupal developers will tell you to use

Drupal. Obviously, if they tell you to use something else, they're not going to get your business. Before looking to hire, you need to understand which platform is best for you, not which is best for the developer.

It's very rare these days that someone would not use a CMS to handle their website. It helps to make simple adjustments and allows content editors to quickly and effectively curate content online. I know many developers who prefer to avoid them, but as a business owner, you need the most effective way to get your content to your audience. That almost never involves waiting for a team to update your website. I've also seen website developers hold business owners ransom over simple updates. Once I was approached and asked if £700 to replace one image on a website was justifiable, to which I answered, "Never!"

One variation of a CMS is the euphemistically—named "DIY Website Builder." These have become very popular due to large advertising budgets and they allow you to build a website without prior knowledge. I highly recommend that you avoid these platforms. The biggest problem is you never actually own your website. Plus, there are ongoing costs, they are limited in design options, and most of the time, you can't access the core code or make adjustments past the basic text on a page. One final point to consider: If the provider that you use stopped trading, then you would lose your website and potentially your business. It's too much of a risk to put your online presence in the hands of another company.

After testing all the major CMS systems, I realised that one stands out as the industry standard. I'm not saying it works every time but the majority of small business owners can use it successfully. At the time of writing this book, over 60 million websites operate on this platform. (That's over 25% of the internet, according to w3techs.com.) I am indeed talking about WordPress.

WordPress is a fantastic CMS. It caters to the majority of users, is very customizable and, because it is open source software and registered under the General Purpose Licence, it can be downloaded from wordpress.org and its core code can be edited as much as you desire.

It's critical to recognise there are two versions of WordPress. There's wordpress.com and wordpress.org. I do not recommend wordpress.com because it is essentially a DIY website builder. Whenever I say WordPress, I'm referring to the standalone .org version.

Lots of people use WordPress even though they aren't very knowledgeable about website development. The platform is built by over 10,000 developers who are continually upgrading and adding to its ability. When you are using WordPress, it's likely that someone has already created the solution to almost every problem you could encounter.

Themes make it possible to fully customize the look and feel of your website. You can use frameworks to create a theme that has a basic design and functions that you can override, or you can purchase a premade theme that does everything out of the box (kind of like the square peg and round hole example). My point is there is a solution for every eventuality and depending on your current situation, you can choose one that suits you.

With WordPress, you have the ability to install a huge variety of programs that plug into the core files. By installing these plugins, you can get all the functionality you can dream of. Whether you need a contact form, a learning management system, affiliate system, forum software, or membership section, the system likely already exists. Of course, WordPress isn't perfect. It is possible for two plugins to conflict with each other. In fact, if your website stops working, the first thing that a developer would do is disable the plugins or ask if you've installed anything new — because often, the problem is a conflict between two plugins. There is an awesome gentleman by the name of Pippin Williamson who has created hundreds of plugins for WordPress. He once said "It's not the quantity of plugins that you have on your website, it is the quality." It only takes one bad plugin to bring your site down. Be very careful about which third−party extensions you rely on to build your website. I provide a list of reputable plugins in the workbook along with tests you can run to ensure you are protecting yourself.

As I said, there are lots of different systems you can use. You don't have to use WordPress, but I do support and use it myself. If you look at my 30−day course, Build Your Website, you'll see it is built on WordPress. I consider it as the benchmark and the way to go forward. It is what I recommend almost everyone use. If you are building something that is very complex and that needs a bespoke system, like a banking system or a gambling platform, then I would not recommend using a CMS and instead go down the custom route.

# Hosting

When you own your website, you are required to host it yourself. We touched on this in Chapter 1 when we related your website to a house. There are enticing offers from DIY website builders to host your website for you but remember that you never really own it and you will never have full access to your systems.

There are also the countless opportunities to use cheap hosting services that appear good but aren't necessarily in your best interest. When you pay one pound a month for your hosting, you are effectively being put onto a server with a group of other people who are all paying the same. This is known as "shared hosting." Let me give you this analogy: If you have a nice, big 10−bedroom house, and you're living there on your own, then you have lots of space and it's very comfortable. Let's imagine we try to cram 1,000 people into that same 10−

bedroom house. Can you see how uncomfortable it's going to be? How many challenges will pop up?

What happens if someone gets ill? We all know how easily the flu spreads and a virus on a shared server is no different. It moves from website to website attacking any weakness it can find — although unlike the flu it's very difficult to know if you have eradicated all traces of a computer virus. They have the ability to lay dormant within your files for a long time.

When you have made sure all the windows are shut on the 10 — bedroom house, then not even a mosquito can get inside. If neighbours leave windows open, there are more chances that bugs can get in. You know how annoying one little mosquito can be! The same thing happens on a server. Each website on the server is effectively a window, and the more websites on the server, the more opportunities for something to come in and attack.

How will people fight for resources and space? When you're using a shared server (which is effectively many people in one house), you are sharing the space with countless other websites. You're now fighting for resources because there is only so much hardware on the server. If your neighbour hogs resources, your website might slow down. And — not if but when — somebody gets a virus, it could potentially affect all of the other websites. The server may even shut down, taking all the websites offline, including yours. If someone is spamming from a website (even without realising it), the whole server could be blacklisted. Consequently, you may get penalised for nothing you've done wrong. Paying one pound a month may seem cheap, but it costs many people much more in time, stress, support and lost business. It's important not to cut corners when you consider your hosting.

You should not only be aware of security, but also consider potential performance issues. When a lot of people use a server, the company running it has a duty to care. That means if you are using excessive resources, they will shut you down to protect everybody else.

When I was living in Wales, I was very fortunate to have one of my websites mentioned on the radio. Chris Moyles ran the Radio 1 breakfast show; it had millions of listeners and they used to play a game on air. He would mention a website and everyone would flock to it. Imagine a hundred thousand people trying to get through the front door of our 10—bedroom house at the same time. That's not going to happen! There's going to be a bottleneck. On a website, when you have too much traffic at the same time, the server will just shut you down to protect the others. After all, if it overloads, it will crash and take everyone offline. Yes I learnt the hard way, which is why I share this story—so you don't have to.

There is no more important time for your website to be online than when you have a sudden influx of visitors. If you were to be mentioned somewhere by a celebrity, there could be a sudden spike in traffic. Or, like has happened to some of my clients, you might do a webinar, host some kind of live video broadcast, or make a live announcement where you ask everyone to click the same link and go to your website. At the moment that you have hundreds of people arriving together, you need to be on a good server that has the resources to support you. Not with one who fails you in the most critical hour.

That said, not all shared servers are bad. There are some really good shared servers out there which I link to in the workbook.

Another option for hosting uses dedicated servers. Dedicated hosting is like living in the mansion on your own. There are pros and cons to this. You've got to maintain that house, so if you buy the server, it is you (or a team you bring in) who has to look after it. I used to run my own servers and I know how challenging and how time—consuming this can be. If you're a business owner, you really don't want to be getting into this.

If however this route is one you want to explore, never give super admin access to anyone. I've heard horror stories about business owners having accounts held ransom or being locked out of their own server.

## Customer Relationship Management (CRM)

I like to think of this as a game that starts the moment visitors land on your website. You can access basic information about them which is sent from their computers — such as IP addresses (which gives their approximate locations), the browsers they are using, what devices they are on and their operating systems. From here, the goal is to collect email addresses. Once acquired, you can create contact records and start to fill in the blanks — first with basic information like their names, moving onto more complex questions relevant to their wants and needs. The more information that you can gather about people who visit your site, the clearer the picture gets about who your customers are. (This circles back to Chapter 2 when we talked about sales funnels and segmenting your list.)

Ultimately, you can use your CRM system to target customers with specific tags and interact with them on a much more personal level. However, CRMs are also very useful to collect all of a customer's tags, items purchased, dates of when they joined and when they bought. Some CRMs even integrate messaging so you can follow the thread back of exactly what a customer has been told.

## Email

I always recommend running your website and your email accounts through separate services. Most people don't consider the possibility of something going wrong but I believe prevention is better than the cure. If your website were to crash for some reason, you would still want your emails to be working. Alternatively, if for some unfortunate reason your email account were hacked and started sending spam, you wouldn't want your website to get blacklisted. Also, if you decided in the future to move your website to another hosting provider, it would be much easier if you didn't have to move your mailboxes with it. These are just a few reasons not to bundle your website and email services with the same company.

Shared hosts offer email as a way to entice users to keep everything on one control panel and it's an attractive concept but the reality is your email and website should never be mixed. A quality website host should focus on being exactly that, not worrying about mail server records. Masterful service providers usually focus on one area, so if you choose the best hosting and email options, you have two services that are maintained by the best in each industry.

## Auto—Responders

Sending emails manually is great, but to get the full potential of automation, you need to explore auto—responders. These systems allow you to configure a sequence of emails that will be sent out at predefined times after people join your list or have a tag applied to their contact records. You create the messages once and every time someone new joins the list, the sequence begins for that person. It's a great way to consistently introduce yourself to new visitors, pre—qualify them and nurture them without constantly being online, writing the same email over and over. An auto—responder is also a great way to segment your list as the qualifying questions you can ask here will allow you to identify automatically who is a good fit for your business, who you can help and those that should be referred elsewhere. It's not about trying to sell to everyone, nor is it about building a massive list, it's about building a quality list that listens to you and responds. The key to achieving this is to make messages feel as personal as possible. Do not just send them out to everyone. Great content here will make the difference on how the relationship is built, which in turn leads to better conversions.

## E—commerce

If you are going to sell a product or service online then you will require a shopping cart. Not only will this allow you to track previous orders and generate reports but it also allows for invoicing, stock control and many other useful features that can make your online shop a success. An ideal e—commerce system is one that integrates with not only your CRM and auto responder but also with your bookkeeping and fulfilment systems.

There are many options for selling online and the first question you need to answer is: Is the product physical or digital? If physical, you should consider fulfilment and how the product is sent. Is this something that would be done in—house, or can you forward the order to a distribution centre?

If you are selling digital products then you need to consider if this product will be delivered via an email or a link on the website. Security is the biggest concern here and knowing how to protect your product is very important. I have seen many people lose sleep and money over trying to protect themselves. If you were my client, I would remind you that if someone wants to steal from you badly enough, they will. Once you accept the fact that not even the biggest corporations in the world are protected from online theft, then you can start to focus on the things that really matter—like nurturing your customers and providing a level of service that no one can match. I always recommend that you protect yourself as best you can, but don't get so hung up on fortifying things that you lose touch with those who matter or lose sight of what you are creating in the first place.

To deliver products online or offline, you not only need the shopping cart but also a way to take payments. For this you use "payment gateways." While the shopping cart holds the chosen products, the payment gateway that is linked to it allows you to transfer the customer's money to your account. Most established shopping carts link into the main payment gateways, although there is often an additional cost for this service.

With any service, you need to identify whether you want to control the process yourself or allow a third party to authorise the transactions for you. Companies such as PayPal offer a fantastic service where they handle all the transactions for a set fee. The customer is directed from your shopping cart to PayPal's website for payment processing and then once successful, is directed back to your website with the tags required for access to the product. It is possible to redirect customers to a specific "Thank you" page once they have purchased and this creates a much better user experience. Integrating personalised messages about the product that customers have just purchased makes your services more professional.

Regardless of whether you get a third—party to process payments or do it on your own site, I recommend that you raise the level of encryption on your site. Installing an SSL certificate is a great way to build trust and rapport. The little green padlock that you see in front of the address in the browser window relates to the SSL (Secure Sockets Layer) certificate which can be purchased and installed on your website. This is not something that many DIY builders offer. If you are selling anything on your site, being able to integrate this is another reason to maintain control of your own website. The SSL certificate not only gives visitors peace of mind that you are established and secure but search engines also favour a website that protect its data. Having an SSL certificate shows responsibility and is something above and beyond what most sites will do.

Tax is another big consideration when selling products online. It makes sense to keep a record for your accounting but also to ensure that the tax is calculated accurately and in a way that makes things easier for your bookkeeping and your business. There are certain laws depending on the country that you are trading from and you need to ensure that you are abiding by them before you start selling online. This often requires adding pages for Terms and Conditions and Privacy Policy that potential customers can read before making a purchase.

## Membership

A popular way to protect digital products or online content is to give access to people once they meet specific criteria. It could be, as mentioned in Chapter 2, that a visitor completed a free registration form to get access to locked content. This way, you collect email addresses for marketing purposes (as long as they agree). Or alternatively, a customer can gain entry to locked areas on your website after purchasing a program. You can charge one-off payments or subscriptions that automatically renew, allowing you control over the content on your website.

A great addition to membership areas is the introduction to gamification. Giving members the ability to earn points, badges or prizes boosts engagement and also rapport. I've seen some amazing marketing campaigns based on this and most people like to play games so introducing a level of fun into your business can help to increase conversions further.

## Support

I often see this section overlooked. At the very least, support is just an email address placed on the website. A step up from this is a contact form but if you have a website and in fact a business, then you should aim to keep your support separate from your main lines of communication. There are many reasons for this. Lots of business owners wear many hats, especially in the beginning. Let's imagine you decide to expand at a later date, or perhaps potential clients and customers are asking a lot of routine questions. If you already have a dedicated support email address, it is that much easier to bring in another person or a team to help with customer support. With a separate channel for support, it's much easier to take yourself out of that part of the equation as you grow.

I see small business owners dealing with support on Facebook chat but the challenge is that their support systems are, again, confined to a third – party system that is beyond control. Your support tickets should be logged in an archive that you can refer back to if needed. It's also a good idea to track your support so you can start to identify challenges and build a knowledge base to support frequently – asked questions. It's much easier to write a reply that you can use again than it is to explain the same thing to multiple people.

Twitter is also well known as a support channel for many large businesses. Customers see that their ability to communicate instantly and have the public transparency of social media ensures that they will get answers to their questions. As a result, many large brands use this platform to their advantage. Publicly dealing with support is not always the answer but it can go a long way towards building trust and credibility if people see that your company actively solves problems.

A support forum on your own website provides a great opportunity that can be run by either an individual or small team. If you build up a following of raving fans then some will help you to moderate the forums and when someone has a problem, you can answer it publicly so that others can see. This way, someone else who may struggle with the same challenge or have the same question could first check the forum and find an answer instantly without the need to use any of your time.

Your customers will go where you educate them to go, but I always suggest the best option is to keep them on your website so you can deal with requests effectively.

# Page Builders

A page builder is effectively a way to build a website without the need to touch code such as HTML or CSS. There is a lot of debate around page builders on the market. Basically, it is a conflict between business owners needing a solution and developers dealing with faulty code which can lead to security vulnerabilities. It's fair to say that when you increase functionality, the ability to create clean code can be affected. An example of this would be the WordPress page builder "Visual Composer" which controls almost half a million websites. Whilst the builder provides amazing functionality, the costs are bugs and unnecessarily bloated code. The developers have set the trend for many other page builders and some are better than others. I give a full breakdown of options as well as my personal preference in the workbook.

# Backing Up Your Website

Here's something to consider. If you get an individual to build your website, what happens if something happens to your developer? What happens to your website? It is critical that you have access to your server and your website, as well as the ability to back it up. If something goes wrong, you must have control.

You must keep backups of your website no matter what platform it's on and you must do that regularly. Don't rely on someone else to back your website up for you. This is too important. Make sure you back your website up yourself and you have a copy yourself. If you have a company or someone else who does it, that's fine. At least once a quarter, ask for the latest copy of the full backup so you can store it yourself, as a failsafe.

# Contact Forms

Have you ever been spammed? If you have your own website that has received the slightest attention, then you will understand the real dilemma of registration, comment and email spam that occurs on a daily basis. I would rather hand over my credit card details than my email address because it's easier to replace my credit card. Think about it. If your email address ends up on a database that is spamming people, there is not much you can do to remove it. You just have to hope that it stops. There are a few things you can do—like close down the account for a few weeks in the hope that it flags you as not active or set up filters to block the incoming messages. I always say that prevention is better than the cure and in the case of email spam, it's often quite simple to protect yourself.

Business owners normally share their email address on their website. Did you know that harmful automated computer programs (bots) can scan websites for anything that contains the @ symbol? When a bot finds an @ sign, it can be automatically added to a database with the text that surrounds it — almost always an email address — and a test email is sent.. If the email gets flagged as delivered, then the email address is moved to a different database where it can be either spammed or sold. Because email tracking is so sophisticated now, it's quite simple to achieve this. It's why I recommend that you never put your email address on your website; instead, use a contact form so that visitors can connect with you safely. When someone completes a form on your website the message is delivered to your email address without compromising your security.

It's also possible to trick these automated spam programs by adding a hidden field in the contact form, otherwise known as a honeypot. This field is not visible to a human visitor thus we do not enter details—but a computer accessing the code fills this honeypot and the message is automatically flagged as spam. You can also initiate simple tests called CAPTCHAs to ensure the person is human. These range from a simple maths question to more complex word or picture challenges to prove that the user is human.

Here are two more reasons that contact forms are a good idea: not only can you configure the default settings so that the sender receives an automated reply after the form is filled out, but you can also follow up with specific questions otherwise known as conditional logic.

"Conditional logic" is when new information is presented, based on a person's previous choice or answer. So on a quiz, for example, our golf coach may ask, "Have you ever played golf before?" If the respondent says YES, a new question, "How many times have you played golf?" could be displayed, whereas if the respondent answers NO, a different question could pop up.

In an auto—responder, with sequences of pre—written emails, it's also possible to predict readers' behaviour and tailor messages based on this.

There are even more benefits to using contact forms! You can ensure that the right team member sees the email, and you also keep your visitors on your website, rather than sending them to their own email where they're likely to be distracted—and may even forget to write to you.

## API Access

Each internet—based application has something called an API (Application Program Interface). By accessing an application's API a developer can make two separate applications talk to each other, thus allowing them to swap information.

An example of this would be an ecommerce system and bookkeeping software. They both perform separate functions and by connecting their APIs, it is possible that, when an order is successfully placed, the bookkeeping software is automatically updated to reflect the current accounts.

# Cookies

Now, these aren't cookies you eat, but rather cookies on websites. In case you have not heard this term before, a cookie stores data about your visit on a particular website. That way, if you ever come back to that website, your information can be accessed.

Have you ever left a shopping cart, and then come back later to find that all your items are still there, waiting for you in your basket? That's because a cookie remembered who you are and what you were doing on that website. Any time you return to a site where you logged in, and when you are not asked to enter your log in details again, you have cookies to thank.

There are laws around using cookies in the EU. It is a legal requirement to announce to your website visitors that you are using cookies. Visitors should be given the option to opt out of having their data stored, even if it affects their user experience.

# Conclusion

It's fair to say that the description in this chapter only just touches the systems that are available. Depending on your profession and business requirements, you may need another system like a gallery, video carousel, webinar platform, or testimonial plugin, just to name a few. The workbook has links and recommendations to get you started. If you have questions, reach out in the Online Mastery community for answers.

# CHAPTER 8
# TESTING

The fact that your website is "built" doesn't mean it's ready for the public. I often see people who are excited share what they have just created without fully testing the systems. It's a mistake to let people use your website if it has not been tested as it makes you look unprofessional, can cause distress and confusion for visitors, and puts undue strain on your support system (which right now needs to focus on the launch, not fighting fires). It's much easier to fix things without the added stress of public awareness.

On Facebook, I belong to a group called Internet Marketing Super Friends. This group has over 10,000 members from beginners to seasoned experts, such as the legendary Frank Kern who is best known for earning over $18 million in just 24 hours. Late one Friday night back in early 2014, a well—known member of the group, who I refer to as Mr X for confidentiality reasons, reached out for help, I seized the opportunity.

Mr X was in the middle of a global launch that he had been working towards for months. His team was running multiple live webinars and driving the traffic to a sales page where people could purchase a digital course. There were hundreds of people on each webinar and the challenge occurred when viewers all tried to access the website at the same time. (Remember the story from Chapter 7 about everyone trying to cram into the house?). As a result, Mr. X's server crashed just 30 minutes before the next webinar. Everybody who tried to visit the website instead received at blank white screen with no access to the website itself. Most visitors in this scenario would either go elsewhere or forget to check back later, resulting in lost sales. To say the least, he was panicking.

The website had been built on a cheap, shared host and it had not been stress — tested. The immense influx of visitors caused the server to overload and crash. Even if we had managed to reboot the server, the same thing would have happened again. That left me just thirty minutes to figure out a solution and implement it.

I decided to adopt two strategies. First, I transferred all the website files to my secure server which I knew could handle the traffic without crashing. However, I couldn't be sure it would work in time since sometimes propagation of a domain name can take up to 24 hours.

As a failsafe, I purchased a new domain name and cloned Mr. X's website. I also set up "load balancing" so that traffic would be diverted between multiple versions of the same site to ease the pressure when the offer was announced in the webinar. His launch continued on time without a hiccup, and he became one of my good clients.

The reason I share this story is because Mr. X estimated a loss of almost $500,000 because he failed to test the systems he was using. It was a loss that could have been avoided with some knowledge and spending an additional $100. It's so important to test the systems and avoid the panic and distress that comes from challenges that WILL occur. If I have learnt one thing, it is that technology is never predictable. I recommend testing two things: the customer journey and website functionality.

# Test the Customer Journey

This is where you should visit your website as a guest for the first time. Imagine you are a member of your target audience and open your website as a guest.

There are many initial things that you will want to check here—from the time it takes the website to load, to the overall look and feel of the website, to spelling and grammar in the emails which get sent out when people opt into your list.

Have you ever signed up on an email list... and then nothing happened? I have opted in to websites but never heard anything ever again. Alternatively, I have been bombarded by ten emails in one morning from the same entrepreneur. Lots of problems come from not testing the sign—up experience prior to launch.

At this stage, you should also purchase your own products. See how the checkout process feels. Is there any friction that might cause someone to leave without purchasing? Once you purchase your product, are you taken to the appropriate page, given correct access and sent an email containing your receipt and instructions on what to do next?

Another great tip I give my clients is to install a chat box onto their websites so that customers can solve any problems (at least for the initial launch). It's a great way for you to get instant access to unforeseen bugs. The last thing customers will do is hunt for contact information when a payment page is not working. Accept that sometimes things may go wrong and give the user as much comfort in reporting this to you.

## Beta Testers

Once you have tested the customer journey, it is advisable to choose a group of people that you can trust (friends, family, and selected members of your target audience) to gain first access to your website. Here, I recommend that you have a constant feed of communication. Give them a brief on actions you want them to take — like purchasing your products, subscribing to your list, etc. — and ask for feedback so you can have real — time examples of users testing your system. This way you have the opportunity to fix any problems that you missed or were too close to notice.

# Test the Functionality

The workbook contains an extensive checklist that you can use before launching your website. Here are the most important things you should consider:

### Cross—Browser Testing

Here we will launch the website on all the main browsers that are supported to check for problems. Developers joke that if it works on Internet Explorer then it's good for anything because of the bugs. Fortunately, Microsoft discontinued the browser, although it's still in existence and is being phased out. The key to understand here is that cross — browser testing is not only about how the website looks on your computer, but how others may view it. Various website browsers deal with things in different ways so make sure it works across them all.

### Cross—Platform Testing

This is similar to browsers but based upon devices. There are more devices on the planet than people. With iOS, Android and so many variations in between, you need to know that your website will work across mobile phones, tablets, laptops, desktops, screen readers and anything else your target audience may use. I can appreciate there may be occasions where bugs appear but you should aim to eliminate the majority before you launch. This will save not only your reputation but as I mentioned before, your support system will be grateful.

### Speed Testing

Performance is one of the biggest considerations. With time being our most valuable commodity and so many businesses competing for our visitors' attention, you have a limited window to make an impact. If that is spent loading your website, then most visitors will give up and leave. Those who stay could have a frustrating experience leading to a negative first opinion. It is wise to run multiple tests to ensure your website is as fast as it can be.

## Code Validation
Search engines notice faulty code in your site and push your site down in the search results. In addition, whilst it might be easy to think you can ignore code because you don't want to live in The Matrix, I can assure you that your security is directly affected by the quality of the code on your website. If you have bugs in your code, your website won't function correctly. It may not perform effectively and it opens you to malicious attacks.

## Support Testing
We have mentioned all the testing on the website and how problems may burden your support channel—but what about the support channel itself? Test to make sure this works the way you want it to, because one of the worst experiences a customer can have is to encounter a problem and have no way to get in touch with you about it.

## Accessibility
This is often overlooked. You need to realize that some people visiting your website might have disabilities and you should cater to them as best you can. Some countries have laws around usability and standards which must be upheld when creating your website.

For a full breakdown of all the tests you should run before launching and a comprehensive checklist, please check the workbook.

# CHAPTER 9
# ANALYTICS

You should give yourself a pat on the back for getting this far. With your website ready to launch, it is almost time to celebrate. But before we do, there is still one more thing to set up if we want to make sure that you are going to be successful online.

We've talked about gathering people's email addresses and building a bigger picture of who they are in your CRM system. What we need to do now is start tracking the way visitors interact with your website. This is known as analytics and it encompasses where people are from, what pages they visit, how long they stay on the page, where they go next, where their mouse is on the screen, where they click. By gathering all this information, we can start to understand which elements of your website are successful, and which are not.

There are two main ways to collect this information. The first is to install some JavaScript code into the header of the website so that visitor behaviour is tracked. This approach was made famous by Google Analytics, which to date is still the most widely used free platform to track website data. The second way we can track visitors is by using "tracking pixels" which are 1x1 transparent square images that get embedded on a visitor's page. Every time someone loads this image by visiting pages, the tracking pixel is installed and activates specific code. Facebook is a good example of a social media website that offers a tracking pixel. They give you the ability to create ads for a custom audience — a list of people who have activated your tracking pixel. Whilst you don't get access to their personal information, you can serve them adverts through the platform and thus keep them engaged after they have left your website.

Once you have analytic tracking set up on your website, it immediately starts to work for whoever lands on your website. You can track in real time where they are in the world based on the IP address they are using. You can tell what language they have set on their computer, what browser and/or device they are using, what operating system they have installed all — before they do anything on your website! Tracking pixels then store a cookie on the visitor's computer so that you can retarget them. I'll talk about that shortly.

If visitors are logged into Google at this point, you can gather additional information that they might have completed when they created their Google account (like gender and general age range, as well as any other public information that they share with the major search engines).

## Retargeting

Have you ever left a website after looking at a product and started to see the same item on various websites or in Google search results? If you have, you know what retargeting is! It's not just on search engines. Social media sites such as Facebook, Twitter and LinkedIn have their own retargeting pixels as well.

You can install a tracking pixel on your website from any of the main social media platforms and that way, if somebody visits your website, the tracking pixel gets activated. You can later run adverts through the social media platforms specifically targeting the people who were on your website. You can even take this one step further by creating specific adverts that get shown depending on which page of your website a customer has visited. Retargeting lets you do lots of clever things, so if someone has been on your website within the last week or month, you can actually serve different messages. That way, you keep them engaged and coming back.

With retargeting, you show up in their awareness again and again. On average, a potential customer needs to be exposed to a product ten times before they are ready to make a purchase decision — unless it's an impulse buy. Retargeting is a very effective way to get your message back into a customer's mind. If they leave, and you don't capture them, it's worthwhile to retarget them.

## Conversion Pixels

This is a type of tracking pixel with a specific purpose. It measures conversions — for example the percentage of visitors who opt—in to your list, or guests who become paying customers. Once they finish a task, they are normally directed to a thank—you page. As with a tracking pixel, the visitor needs to actually visit the page where the pixel is for it to be activated.

Let's imagine you want to know what percentage of people actually sign up for your opt—in gift, or buy a product. To do this, you need to measure and compare visitor traffic over a series of pages. If 100 people visit the signup form (and activate a tracking pixel there) and only 25 people reach the thank—you page (which has its own conversion pixel), then you know your opt—in process is converting 25% of your visitors.

Over time, you have a better idea of what's effective and what's not. Once you have information, you can test possible improvements and make adjustments. We cover "split—testing" in more detail in Chapter 10, but it's like I said at the beginning: your website is about constant and never—ending improvement. Remove what doesn't work, and improve what does. That way, your online presence becomes more effective, which leads to more success.

## Tag Management

A very simple and efficient way to manage all your pixels and scripts is to install a tag manager. This lets you install just one piece of code on your website. Tag manager software has a central dashboard where the script for each of your different tracking and conversion pixels can be installed and maintained. This allows you to choose which pages the pixels are active on.

## Heat Map Tracking

This allows you to track visitors' mouse pointers on their screens. (Or, if somebody is on a touch device, you see where they touched.) You can see how far somebody scrolls down a given page or what buttons they click. Keep in mind this information is anonymous — what you see is "what" a visitors does on your site not "who" does it.

From the dashboards of heat map tracking programs, you can literally see what works and what doesn't. A heat map gives you a fully visual representation of how your web pages are being used. The program can actually record the visitors' mouse movements. Wherever their mouse is pointing is usually where they're looking. This is particularly useful for your landing pages, so that you know what elements work, and what elements don't.

# Conclusion

If this seems overwhelming, just realise that I've highlighted the tip of the iceberg. I've given you the most important analytics tools to pay attention to — so get started, and when these are fully functional, you can explore the deeper layers under the water.

One final word on this subject: get the analytics and tracking software set up as early as possible. And remember that all of this data on its own is worthless without interpretation. Once the tracking has been set up, either you or an agency you hire should review that data, assess it, and then act upon it to make consistent improvements in maximizing your customer journey.

# CHAPTER 10
# SPLIT TESTING

You made it this far! Your site is live. You are getting traffic and you are monitoring your data. But how do you know what is effective and what is not?

The best way to know for certain is to "split test." That means making two or more variations of a page, so that you can send a percentage of traffic to each one over a period of time and see which one performs the best. You can split—test anything:

- Prices
- Text
- Videos
- Images
- Headlines

or anything else you can think of. The page we start with is called the "control" (the current and active version that live traffic visits). Based on that, you can create as many variations as you want, although I personally recommend split—testing no more than two variations at a time.

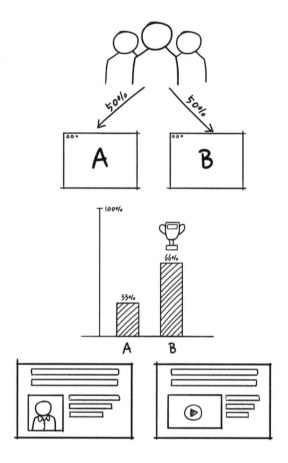

When you create variations, it's important to change only one thing at a time so that you know what is responsible for the results. If you were to change multiple elements on a page, you would not know which is responsible for the change in your results and therefore the results will not be conclusive. Split testing is never finished. You should always be testing to try to improve the conversions on your website.

Because you have to gather enough data for your results to be relevant, split tests can only work when you are driving traffic to a website. The accuracy of a test depends on the number of people that participate. If you have a split test running for 30 days that only tracks 10 visitors, the statistics you collect won't be as accurate as ones from a split test that runs for 30 minutes and attracts 1000. I would suggest at a minimum you use 100 visitors as a base for your tests.

It's nothing more than a numbers game and the more people who are sent through your test, the more accurate the statistics. One common approach is to split the traffic 50 / 50 between your control and one variation. Just change one element on your website and monitor it. The more data you can correlate during a set timeframe the more accurate the results will be.

You can then determine the winner based on the results you are tracking. It may be how many people clicked a button or scrolled down past the top of the page. You could track how long someone stays on a page. The options are up to you and marketers are always creating new ways to be clever.

A great example of split testing is identifying the best price for your product. For this test we pick a control price of £100. We create two variations. One at £50 and one at £150. We then send a third of the traffic to each price point and see which one converts the most people.

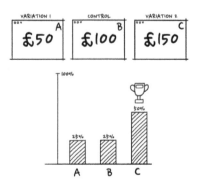

As you can see from the results, £150 (Variation 2) is the clear winner. We now want to run a second test to refine our understanding further.

We keep £100 as the control and the winner from the last test but introduce a new mid range variation. As you can see, we find that £125 is a better performing price and can now become our new control. The idea is to keep testing until we find the perfect price that our target audience are happy to pay.

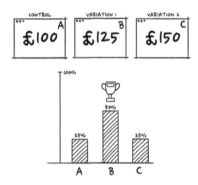

Ultimately, split—testing gives you the certainty that people are interacting with your content and responding to your calls to action. It removes the speculation that comes from what you *think* works and replaces it with the facts regarding what *actually* works. This information is vital to your success.

Testing isn't limited to your website, you can split test everything from adverts and promotions to emails that are sent out nurturing your customers. You should always be looking at ways to improve your online presence. Remember in the words of Tony Robbins, Constant and Never Ending Improvement — CANI.

# WHAT'S NEXT?

## Congratulations!

You now have a solid understanding of the foundation required to plan a website that gets results. My recommendation now is that you review this book as a reference whilst completing the workbook.

## Workbook Download

Please visit

http://PlanYourWebsite.co.uk/workbook

or scan the QR code below
to download your FREE workbook.

Once you have completed your strategy, you or a member of your team can follow our online course, Build Your Website to implement everything you have learnt here. This book teaches you what you need to do and the online course shows you how to do it step — by — step. At the end of the course, you will have built your own website and set up everything that was mentioned in this book. If you don't have time or the desire to build your own website, you can give your strategy to a professional team who can create your vision or speak to us at Online Mastery where we are happy to assist you further.

Whether this is the start or end of our journey together, I just want to thank you. I am truly grateful for your time spent reading this book. I gave it everything I have and I really want it to serve you in a positive way.

Take what works. Leave what does not and please reach out with your feedback. I would love to hear from you.

To your success,

Steve Woody
https://onlinemastery.co.uk


P.S. If you enjoyed this book and found it valuable please take the time to visit Amazon and leave feedback. Your experience will help to serve others who are looking to create a business online and need guidance to ensure they have the best information available to them.

P.P.S. The next step in your journey should be to create your website. To help you with this I have created an online course that takes you through everything you will need step by step to apply the theory you have learnt in this book.

You can continue your journey at

https://onlinemastery.co.uk/build-your-website

Lightning Source UK Ltd.
Milton Keynes UK
UKHW021354070819
347544UK00009B/161/P